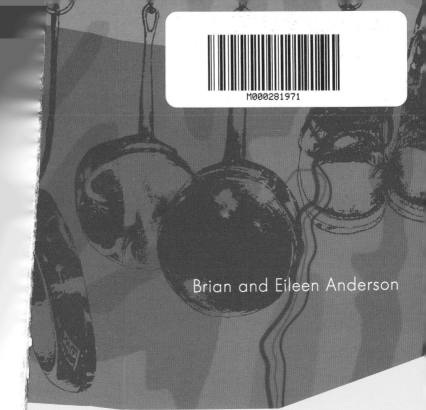

Brian and Eileen Anderson

walk & eat
KEFALONIÁ

CONTENTS

If holidays are about new experiences, then this pocket guide will add a further dimension to your stay on Kefaloniá. It solves two problems — where to walk and where to find some good, traditional food. The gastronomical touch extends a little further, with recipes for some of the island's dishes, both specialities and traditional. There are strolls for hot days and longer walks to work up an appetite. If you're just after some recommendations for where to eat, look no further!

Highlights at a glance
- 10 day walks, each with topographical map
- 2 excursions — one a walking tour around Argostóli and the other to Itháca, the land of Odysseus
- recommended restaurants for the walks
- recipes to try out when self-catering or back home
- hints on wheat-, gluten- and dairy-free eating and cooking on the island

INTRO

THE WALKS

The walks in this book vary in length and difficulty. None is too strenuous and all can be done by a reasonably fit walker. The walks are spread around the island and there is at least one near every major resort. The island's bus service is good but limited, depending on where you choose to stay, but a hire car will give you best access to all the walks.

There isn't a great deal of walking information available for Kefaloniá and this book brings together 10 of the best walks.

THE EXCURSIONS

Argostóli, capital of the island, is built for pleasure. A broad promenade, fishermen selling their early-morning catch, the best fruit and veg market on the island, a shoppers' haven along the first stone-paved street on the island, aptly called Lithó-stroto and now pedestrianised, great eating places, the best museums and everything to make this excursion a great day out.

The second excursion travels by car ferry over a 'wine-dark sea' to the nearby mountainous island of Itháca. Check out the picturesque ports and sleepy villages and, for the romantics, places associated with Homer's hero, Odysseus, King of Itháca. Easily achieved on a day trip.

THE RESTAURANTS AND TAVERNAS

We have featured only restaurants where we have dined and which meet our guidelines. Obviously, an important tourist destination like Kefaloniá has many excellent restaurants catering for different tastes. We have not included those offering 'international cuisine' — dishes like peppered steaks and chicken Kiev, no matter how good they may be. Similarly, Chinese and Indian restaurants do not feature.

Our aim has been to find restaurants and tavernas serving good, traditional Greek food using fresh ingredients. Many restaurant owners are keen to advertise a 'Greek Cuisine' and yet you may find only a tiny corner on the menu for traditional Greek dishes.

Restaurants and tavernas differ largely in presentation. In a restaurant you expect to find the table set with a tablecloth, cutlery and wine glasses laid out ready, as you would

Price guide

Restaurants and tavernas aren't graded or classified by the tourist authorities as they once were, and are no longer subject to price controls. In spite of this, the prices between the various establishments remain surprisingly similar. The price guides in this book (€ to €€€) indicate 'very reasonable' to 'fairly pricey'. Remember that this guide relates not to prices at home, but to *prices on Kefaloniá* and is a comparison between the various tavernas and restaurants. The majority fall into the average category indicated by €€. Even so, it's always possible to enjoy a relatively inexpensive meal in a top restaurant by choosing carefully from the menu. There's usually a large choice of cheaper starter dishes which can easily make up a satisfying meal.

in any restaurant. Expectations in a taverna are a little different. Shortly after sitting down, a plastic-backed paper table cloth will appear and be laid over the tablecloth, fixed with side clips. The cutlery arrives wrapped in a paper napkin (it used to arrive in the bread basket, but bread is no longer served automatically. Wine is drunk from small glasses, although wine glasses may make an appearance. But other than in presentation, there is little difference, the food may well be very similar in quality and price. Restaurants have grown out of tavernas and are only likely to be found in the larger towns.

Taverna sign

Even in the more expensive restaurants it's still easy to enjoy a good meal by choosing carefully. The Greek menu offers so many starters, like the well-known Greek salad, taken together with *tzatzíki* and a jug of house wine, and you will certainly not need to raid the piggy bank to end up with a good light lunch.

Please be aware that no restaurant or taverna has paid in cash or in kind to be included in this guide.

THE RECIPES

Requests for recipes always brought a delighted and enthusiastic response. Then the difficulties started. Take a handful of this and a cup of that or take 12 eggs and so on. Weights and measures are quite foreign to them. One interesting aspect was drawing out of the chefs their preferred herbs. Traditional recipes passed down through the family use only local herbs which grow naturally or are grown commercially on the island. Chief of these is parsley, which is used in so many recipes as a flavouring or as decoration. Oregano and dill are commonly used, but spices feature far less often.

Many standard recipes can vary quite considerably. Kefalonian meat pie is a good example. Each one we tried and each recipe we acquired was different. Basically, it's a mix of meat and rice in a pie. Different size of meat cuts, different ratios of meat and rice, different herbs and spices were among the variations and, in one case, lentils replaced rice. Two tips from the Greeks when cooking dried beans. The first tip is, after soaking, bring to the boil, drain, and boil again in fresh water. This helps reduce flatulence. Secondly, to keep the skins tender, add the olive oil and salt five minutes before the end of cooking.

So we have drawn all our information together and tried to make the dishes at home to recapture the taste and flavour. It's difficult without exactly the same ingredients and, without the intangibles — the sunshine, the holiday atmosphere, the waves lapping on the sea shore — it's doubly difficult. Even so, the recipes are authentic and results pleasing.

Olive oil isn't good to use for frying at high temperatures, the lighter sunflower oil or similar is more commonly used by

Acknowledgements

We would like to thank Nick and Vivian Sklavounaki of Vivian Villa (www.villavive @otenet.gr), our regular base in Argostóli, who have become good friends over the years as we researched our *Visitors Guide to Kefalonia* (now a Kindle edition). They have helped with our research on previous occasions, but this time Greek cooking was in the spotlight. Viv is a great cook, as we well know, so special thanks to her for tips and recipes. Also to Liana Sklavounaki for checking our Greek. Vivian Villa also has new superior apartments by the sea at Fanari Beach (Walk 1).

the Greeks for this purpose. If cooking at home, rape seed oil is as healthy as olive oil and better for frying. The Greeks tend to use olive oil excessively but the quantities have been reduced in our recipes.

EATING GREEK

Eating out for Greek families is a social occasion. It's a pleasure just to watch them. Family and friends gather around the table, men and women mostly choosing to segregate themselves, with the children up and down as

children are. When the food arrives, it's placed in the centre of the table for all to share. Plate after plate arrives until there's hardly room left. The chatter is long and loud, and the pace of eating is slow. Hot food cooling is of no concern. If it's a festive occasion, impromptu Greek dancing quite often follows.

Visitors, on the other hand, usually order a Greek salad for one person, perhaps a *tzatzíki* for another and so on. But there are so many different dishes and flavours to enjoy, it makes sense to **put all the starters in the middle and share**. If you indicate that you would like to eat this way, the waiter will

Selection of starters at Arkondikó in Argostóli: roasted aubergine salad, battered courgettes and, behind, *riganáda* (see page 44)

bring a plate for each person. Even with only two of you dining, two or three starters can be tried — but it's even better with four or more people eating. After the starters, it's much more acceptable to order individual main courses, although these can be treated in the same way as *mezédes* (appetizers) and shared. We became so used to sharing when living in Greece that we now often share starters and sweets — even in restaurants at home.

After decades of tourism, many tavernas now appreciate that you may not want every course you order to arrive at the same time. But some, especially in country areas, may *not* understand this, so it is best to order *mezédes* first, then order the rest later — or say *argótera* (later) for main courses, etc.

The Greeks **order certain dishes by weight**, usually lamb, pork chops or *kalamári* — all of which will be ordered by the kilo. A half kilo is usually plenty for two people and can be cheaper than ordering by the portion. Fish almost always appears on the menu priced by the kilo. It sometimes looks very expensive when you see the kilo price, but the fish will be weighed and a portion size is usually 300-400 g. If the fish you have chosen is particularly large, the waiter will weigh it for you and tell you its cost to get your agreement.

KEFALONIAN FOOD

Kefalonian food follows traditional Greek cuisine but not necessarily the full spectrum of dishes and there is one speciality not widely found elsewhere, Kefalonian meat pie. The island is famous for its *féta* cheese which is said to have originated on Kefaloniá. Strangely enough, there is no factory of any size on the island making it and production is left in the hands of the various villages. The result is that no two *fétas* taste the same!

Manéstra

Over the many years we've been travelling to Greece and enjoying Greek food, the cuisine has always remained traditional and constant but there are now signs of change. Cooking programmes on Greek television are bringing a more progressive influence to the cuisine, and traditional dishes are starting to evolve. At the moment this is most noticeable in the salads which are improving in variety and content. Balsamic vinegar, an influence from its close connection with Italy, is a recent introduction on Kefaloniá.

One quick and easy hot one-pan meal we *do* make in self-catering (and often at home) uses a rice-like pasta, *manéstra*. On Kefaloniá, this is also known by its Italian name, *orzo*. Look for it in the pasta section on supermarket shelves. It looks just like rice and comes in three sizes, small *(mikró)*, medium *(métrio)* and large *(megálo)*. Greek friends recommend the medium size for general use. Look for *kritharáki métrio* or the Italian *orzo medio,* both names under the *manéstra* umbrella. If you make this at home, however, you'll have to bring packets of pasta home from Greece unless you live near a Greek produce supplier or specialist delicatessen. Below is our basic 'throw together' recipe; experiment with it and come up with your own variations. We prefer *manéstra* to rice, as it absorbs flavours beautifully and is so easy to use. But, naturally, if you need a gluten-free option, it's a good recipe for a *risotto*.

Using 50-75 g of pasta per person, select some pre-cooked diced meats (chicken, turkey, pork, etc) and vegetables suitable for a stir fry (chopped onion, garlic, peppers, courgettes, celery, broccoli florets, frozen peas … whatever). Heat olive oil or sunflower oil in a large frying pan/wok, and gently stir fry the *fresh* vegetables with the pasta briefly. Then dissolve a stock cube or two in 250 ml water and stir into the pan. Add more water if necessary. Cover and simmer for 6 min. Stir and check the water, then add seasoning, herbs, the meat and the *frozen* peas (if used). Cover, bring back to a simmer, and cook a further 5 min. The pasta should be soft if the dish is ready and the moisture absorbed. Serve on its own or with crusty bread and green salad.

THE MENU

Menus *(katálogos)* have become more helpful. Restaurants now give some indication of the contents of a dish and unusally indicate dishes that contain ingredients cooked from frozen.

The latter is done usually by adding an asterisk or the word *katef*, short for *katepsegménos*.

Life would be simpler if the menu in Greece was always set out in the familiar way of starters, main courses and sweets. It sometimes is, but then often further divided or subdivided. Fortunately, menus are usually available in English — although some are still not always as helpful as they might be. A number of dishes have no direct equivalent. *Hórta (xórta)*, for example, is a dish variously described as boiled greens or spinach. It's the green leaves of the dandelion family (but not strictly dandelions), sometimes collected wild, which are boiled, strained, seasoned, amply tossed in olive oil and lemon juice and served as a single vegetable dish. On Kefaloniá there is a similar dish, called *tsigaridiá*. Very good if it's fresh — a great favourite with the Greeks, and one of our favourites too. Similarly, familiar dishes such as *mousakás* are described in all sorts of ways — 'meat pie with béchamel sauce' is fairly typical.

Hórta

The **starters** (*orektiká*) make up the most interesting section, and the list should be quite long. Salads are usually listed here, but may appear in their own section; the same is true for cheese dishes. Starters are a boon for vegetarians and vegans and often suitable for those on gluten-free diets, since many are vegetables served as single dishes — for instance giant butter beans (*gígantes*), beetroot cooked with their leaves (*patzária*), fried courgettes (*kolokithákia*

13

Boiled vegetables (above) and tzatzíki

tiganitá), fried aubergines (*melitzana tiganitá*) and the already-mentioned *hórta*. Boiled vegetables (usually courgettes and green beans) may not sound appealing, but can be beautifully presented and delicious with lemon and olive oil or a dip.

There's an interesting array of **dips** — from the familiar *taramasaláta* (cod's roe) and *tzatzíki* (yoghurt/cucumber/garlic) to aubergine dip (*melitzanosaláta*) and garlic/mashed potato (*skordaliá or aliátha*). On Kefaloniá *skordaliá* is often served to complement other dishes, particularly cod fish. These dips sometimes appear under the salad list.

Surprisingly, **soups** are a common feature on Kefalonian menus — usually bean, lentil, meat and vegetable. Another Kefalonian special, often seen on the menu as 'mushed eggs', is *strapetsáda*. This is scrambled **eggs** in spicy sauce with *féta* cheese.

Cheese (*tirí*) dishes on the starters list include *féta* sprinkled with herbs and drizzled with olive oil, *saganáki* (fried *féta* — or another cheese), *saganáki sto foúrno* (oven-baked *féta* with tomatoes and peppers, often spicy), grilled *haloúmi* (a dish borrowed from Cyprus), *tirosaláta* (a spicy cheese dip), and *tirokeftédes* (cheese croquettes).

Greek **salad** *(horiátiki saláta)* is synonymous with Greek cuisine for most visitors. There is no standard; it depends on the season, but tomato, cucumber and olives are ever-present, topped by a lump of *féta* cheese and often liberally soaked in olive oil and vinegar. Sometimes it can be a meal in itself. It's on every menu and serves as a useful price comparison between tavernas. Very often we prefer just to have a salad of tomato and cucumber *(domáta/angoúri).* One salad mostly ignored by visitors, but popular with the Greeks, is lettuce salad *(maroúli saláta).* It doesn't sound very exciting, but is really tasty the way it's prepared. Salads are slowly evolving, cherry tomatoes replacing or supplementing the large Mediterranean tomato, rocket leaves and roasted aubergine adding much more variety.

The **main courses** are listed under *entrádes,* grills and/or meat *(kréas),* or there may be just one list. Normally, under the *entrádes* you can expect to find **Greek specialities** like *mousakás, stifádo* (a veal and shallot stew), *kokkinistó* (veal stew with tomatoes) and *giouvétsi* (veal in a clay pot with *manéstra,* the rice-like pasta mentioned on page 11); the **grills** are found in other sections. **Fish** *(psári)* or **seafood** *(thalasiná)* are normally listed separately.

Beef is served in the form of veal *(moskári)* — beef from a milk-weaned yearling animal. Steaks seem to appear on restaurant menus, whereas tavernas stick with chops *(brizóla)* which are large and meaty. Pork chops *(hoiriní brizóla)* and lamb cutlets *(païdákia)* are popular, but these meats are also served on skewers as *souvláki.* Chicken and fish are also sometimes served this way. Goat *(katsíki)* is popular on Kefaloniá, and is eaten as chops or a roast which, like lamb, can be ordered by the kilo or by the portion (merída).

Poultry is almost invariably chicken (kotópoulo), but turkey (galópoula) is found occasionally, as well as rooster/cockerel.

On a visit to a good supermarket or a market, you will see fresh vegetables in abundance, but you are unlikely to see many **vegetables** with your main course — if any. Chips are fairly ubiquitous, but some dishes like squid (kalamári) are served without, so you may need to enquire. Chips (patátes tiganités) are always available as a side order with your starters or main course. If you just ask for patátes, it's generally understood you want chips. In one or two tavernas on Kefaloniá, particularly in Argostóli, there is often a choice of potato — from chips to boiled or jacket.

It's fairly typical to find **fish restaurants around coastal regions**. Although predominantly serving fish, fish restaurants invariably offer a selection of meat dishes. Kalamári is always popular, especially with the Greeks. Fresh is always best, tastier and more succulent, but not always available. Frozen can be good but more variable in quality. Octopus (xtapódi) is usually offered as grilled or cooked in wine or vinegar. Swordfish (ksifías), salmon (solómos), salt cod (bakaliáros), and shrimps (garídes) are regulars on the menu. Of the smaller fish, maridáki and atheriná reach the menu in September, sardines (sardéles) and gavros are summer season dishes. Gavros is translated as anchovy, but they are most definitely *not* anchovies.

Desserts are listed under glyká, which means 'sweet'. The Greeks have a sweet tooth and love their sweets soaked in syrup and honey. But these sweets are not a major feature of taverna menus and sometimes don't appear at all. Very often the taverna owner will bring complementary fresh fruit, depending on the season. It might be grapes, watermelon or oranges, but one of our favourites is sliced apple dusted with cinnamon and drizzled with honey. Restaurants usually offer a better menu for desserts.

One of the most popular sweets with tourists is yoghurt and honey which may be topped with walnuts. It's not really a traditional Greek sweet, but a response to its immense popularity with visitors. Even if not on the menu, it can often be rustled up for you, since the taverna is likely to have a stock of thick, strained yoghurt for making *tzatzíki*.

Baklavá, *kataïfi* and *halvá* are amongst the intensely sweet sweets. *Baklavá*, multi-layered filo pastry

Baklavá with ice cream at Ta Pitharia in Skála (page 134)

sandwiching finely chopped almonds or walnuts, rich in butter and soaked in sugar/honey syrup, finds many devotees (125 g = 695 calories). *Kataïfi*, best described as small shredded wheats (actually a pastry), soaked in sugar/honey syrup appeals to the same group of supporters, as does the *halvá*, a brown, sugar-rich sesame seed confection which is poured into a mould to set. *Galaktoboúriko* comes in much lower down the calorie scale. It's vanilla custard sandwiched between layers of filo pastry. *Lou-koumádes*, batter balls soaked in honey syrup, is another sweet.

Frappé

In the heat of summer this is a popular drink for Greeks as well as tourists. Easy to make yourself, either in one of the cheap plastic *frappé* shakers (available in supermarkets) or in a jar with a screw cap. For each *frappé*, put a teaspoon of instant coffee in the container, add ice cubes then half water and half milk. You can use fresh milk or soya. Add sugar if wanted. Shake vigorously until the coffee has dissolved and it's nice and frothy. Iced chocolate is very popular now as well: if you're making it yourself, substitute cocoa (and sugar) or drinking chocolate for the instant coffee.

Coffee *(kafé)* deserves a special mention. At one time, only 'Nes' (short for Nescafé or any instant coffee) was available: strong enough to 'stand up' the proverbial spoon, it was served with a glass of water. Nowadays, water is still often served, but other options such as filter and cappuccino are commonplace. *A word of caution:* Greek Nes (Nescafé) is stronger and more bitter than its UK equivalent, so use it sparingly when you buy it for use at your hotel or in self-catering.

If you do happen to be in an establishment which only serves Nes, and you're not a lover of very strong coffee, ask for it *elafrí*, weak. Another pitfall to watch out for is added sugar. The Greeks normally have sugar in their coffee, which is sometimes added automatically when it's made. As well as *elafrí*, you need to add *horís zákari* (without sugar). You may require your coffee with/without milk *(me/horís gála)*.

Ordering a **Greek coffee** is quite different. Sugar is added during the preparation, so you need to specify *glykó* (sweet), *métrio* (medium) or *skéto* (without sugar). Greek coffee is never served with milk.

Tea *(tsái)* is widely available — even herbal teas — in restaurants and some cafés.

KEFALONIAN WINES

Vines are grown extensively on Kefaloniá, especially in the Omalá Valley, around St Gerasímos Monastery, and there are a good number of wine producers on the island. The most important grape variety is the *robola*, a Kefalonian speciality, which produces a refreshing, medium-bodied white wine with hints of citrus. This is sold in the shops as Robola from Cephalonia. Other grapes for white wine include *tsaoussi*, *zakyntho*, *vosilidi* and muscat. Red wines are generally not of the same quality, and the most commonly used grape here is *mavrodaphne*. One of the best reds we found is sold as Linos.

Be sure to visit the Robola Winery when you're near Valsamáta (Walk 3).

In spite of the best efforts of the wine producers to promote the leading labels, the bulk wine released for sale as house wine is virtually the same standard. It's so good and so much cheaper that everybody drinks it, and we have yet to have a house wine, especially white, on Kefaloniá that disappointed us.

House wines are bought by the kilo, which is effectively the same as a litre. It's a hangover from the days when you went along to the shop with your jug to buy wine from the barrel. For four people your first order would be a kilo, but two might start with a half-kilo (*misó kilo*) and take it from there.

RETSINA, OÚZO — AND BEER

It's said that resinated wine, or retsína, originated in the days before wine bottles, when wine was stored in jars or skins sealed with pine resin. When bottles came on the scene, the wine without the resin flavour was not universally popular, so retsína was born. It's generally much preferred by the Greeks — but less so on Kefaloniá, possibly because the quality of the house wines is so good. Provided the wine is only lightly resinated, it can be quite palatable, and the resin stabilises the wine — which gives it consistency. Our favourite is Malamátina. Kourtáki is the best-known brand internationally, but this is moderately resinated and not the easiest retsína for the uninitiated to fall in love with at first sip! Often a pale-coloured retsína signifies less resin, making a more palatable drink for first-timers.

Oúzo is a drink for bright sunshine and bonding, Greek-style. This aniseed-flavoured drink is taken with ice and water and, traditionally, a few nibbles. There are still one or two *oúzeri* around, where you can sit with an oúzo and expect some free *mezédes* (*mezés* for short) — a little plate with a piece of cheese perhaps, a chunk of bread, maybe a few cold chips, or anything to hand. But this tradition is now only usually found in country villages — well away from areas frequented by mass tourism.

When we lived on Lesvos some years ago, the locals insisted that Lesvos made the best oúzo in Greece. We put this down to local pride, but since then we have travelled to many other Greek islands and, sure enough, everybody tells us the best oúzo is from Lesvos. Oúzo 12, Mini and Barbayanni are all leading brands.

Tsiperou is a strong clear spirit.

One or two international **beers** are available, but Mythos, Alpha, Fix and Amstel, lager-type beers, are freely available, both bottled and draught, and suit the sunny hot weather well.

PLANNING YOUR VISIT
When to go

Although one or two hotels in Argostóli remain open all year, Kefaloniá is effectively closed for tourism in winter. Lids come off the paint tins in April, when work starts and the island comes to life to get ready for the new season. This is about the earliest time that can be considered, although getting there will mean taking an international flight to Athens and an internal flight to Kefaloniá, often called Kafaliniá on airport departure boards — a journey which can usually be achieved in one day. Direct charter flights start in May and continue until early October.

The best time for walkers is in the **spring and autumn** months. Late April/May is a great time to be there walking. The temperature isn't too high, and the spring flowers are a definite bonus. The heat starts to build quickly in June, and at some point it becomes too hot to enjoy strenuous walks — but some of the easy or short walks remain possible, especially with an early start. July, August and early September are generally too hot for walkers unless you are prepared to rise with the sun and walk very, very early in the morning. Walking in the full heat of the sun in this period is risking serious heat exhaustion and is *most definitely not recommended.* Temperatures decline slowly throughout September, and usually by the middle of the month, walking is back on the agenda — but it may still be advisable to avoid strenuous walks for a time. By October the temperatures are usually back to the mid or low 20s and walking becomes a pleasure again.

But eating is a pleasure to be enjoyed any time of the year so, even if it's too hot to walk, you might still want to try some of our suggested restaurants and tavernas!

Where to stay

Our preferred base is **Argostóli** simply because it lies at the hub of the island and is well served by public transport. It has no beach, which will not please a lot of people, but it's not far from Lássi and a number of beaches. Argostóli has the only sizeable fruit and vegetable market on the island, and the town offers some of the best eating, although not everywhere is good.

Moving around the island counter-clockwise from Argostóli:

Lássi, very much a ribbon development along the main road, has a selection of good beaches and is a popular resort. It also has the advantage of being very close to Argostóli, close enough to walk the short main road route (2km) or the longer old carriageway route which is one of our featured walks.

Lourdáta: features in many brochures and has a good beach, but is a quieter, isolated resort; a hire car will be essential to see anything of the island, since there is a limited bus service.

Kateliós, another small resort with plenty of character, is also isolated, but at least lies on the bus route.

Skála: has developed into the island's leading resort. A huge sandy beach with plenty of space, a wide choice of tavernas and restaurants, good shopping and a walk on the doorstep.

Póros: lots of scenic character being nudged into the sea by the mountains, but losing out to neighbouring Skála. Mass tourism to Póros has declined. There are no taxis now, but there *are* buses during the season. There are places to eat and at the port which we feature for our two Póros walks. Ferries ply back and forth from this port to Killíni (a good connection for ferries to Zákynthos) and Pátras, both on the Peloponnese mainland.

Sámi: another major ferry port with a wide sea-front captured by tavernas and restaurants. Much of the accommodation lies back from the town, sometimes a fair distance. Its beach lies on the Karavómilos side or, if you are prepared to walk (3.5km) or take a taxi, you can visit the stunning white shingle beach of Antísamos. We feature a good footpath walk up to ancient Sámi from here.

Ag Efimía: This attractive but low-key fishing village and yachting centre is growing steadily in popularity. It has no beach to write home about. Some walking information is displayed on a board in the harbour to help you across the neck of the island to Mírtos beach on the other coast. Not all, but

House in Ássos

much of this walk is along the main road.

Fiskárdo: this delightful yachting harbour enclosed by pastel-coloured houses is a gem of a place to visit. Endless restaurants and tavernas spread around the quayside keep the place buzzing by day and lend a charming atmosphere to the evening. As a place to stay it's rather small, with a tiny town beach and a larger, shingle beach not too far away. We feature a fairly lengthy walk from here which can be used just to reach the shingle beach at Émblissi and visit on an excursion.

Ássos: another place of charm and character visited on one of our walks. It lies on the neck of a peninsula overlooked by a Venetian castle. A hire car is helpful here.

What to take

There is no special dress code for dining, except that shorts are not always appreciated in restaurants and some tavernas during the evening.

It's more important to concentrate on packing suitable walking gear. Walking boots are the footwear we most strongly recommend, but not all the walks demand them. Some of the track walks are fairly easy underfoot, and for these we prefer **walking shoes**, specialist walking trainers or sandals, especially if the weather is hot. Each person should carry a **small rucksack** and it's advisable to pack it with a **sunhat**, **suncream**, **first-aid kit** and some extra **warm clothing**. A **long-sleeved shirt** and **long trousers** should be worn or carried for sun protection and for walking through spiny vegetation. You should always carry a **mobile phone**; the **emergency number** on Kefaloniá (as throughout the EU) is 112.

Depending on the season, you may also need lightweight **rainwear** and a lightweight folding **umbrella** (which can also be useful for sun protection on sun-exposed sections of a walk). Some of our walks end up at a beach, so **swimwear** could be usefully included. A reliable litre-size **water bottle** is well worth packing, although small, easily carried bottles of water can be bought all over the island. *It is imperative that each walker carries at least a half-litre of water — a full litre or more when the weather is hot.*

Planning your walks

Look over the walks you plan to take in advance, to check out **transport**. There may be a walk or two on your doorstep and, depending where you stay, one or two more may be reached by public transport but the remainder will require a hire car or taxi.

We have **graded** the walks with the weekend walker in

mind, based on an ambient temperature *below the mid 20s C.* When temperatures rise above this level, walkers expend more energy simply keeping cool, and uphill walking especially is much more tiring. The **walking times** given at certain points always refer to the total walking time from the start and are based on an average rate of 4km per hour and allowing an extra 15min for every 100m/330ft of ascent. These time checks are not intended to predetermine your own pace, but are meant to be useful reference points. A walk might easily take you *twice as long* if you dawdle over the scenery, nature-watch or stop for the thousand little reasons which bring walkers to a halt.

The best **map** of the island is the 1:65,000 Anavasi map, available on the island or from your usual stockist. Our 1:50,000 walking maps, originally based on an old Road Editions map, have been very heavily updated by our work in the field. Note that the only paths on our maps are those we *know* to be viable. Free **GPS track** downloads are available for all these walks: see the *Walk & eat Kefalonia* page on the Sunflower website. *Even if you don't use GPS, it's great fun opening the files in Google Earth and previewing the walks in advance.*

Walking safely depends in great part on *knowing what to expect and being properly equipped*. For this reason we urge you to read through the *whole* walk description at your leisure *before* setting out, so that you have a mental picture of each stage of the route and the landmarks. One or two of these walks are waymarked, and **waymarks** may be found along parts of the others. *But beware: waymarks are not always maintained, so always follow our route description or refer to our GPS downloads.*

Thunderstorms in late autumn, after a long summer drought, can cause **flash flooding**, potentially a serious danger to walkers. Keep an eye on the forecast at this time of the year and do not take risks with the weather.

ON ARRIVAL
Tourist information
Not all resorts have a Tourist Information Office, but one can be found in Argostóli and Sámi.

Bus timetables are usually available at the tourist offices (or online), but see under 'Transport' below.

Motorists picking up a hire car should be aware of a potentially dangerous system on roundabouts: at the moment drivers have to *stop when on a roundabout* to give way to traffic entering from the right. Re-check this on arrival. The best touring **map** is the Anavasi map cited opposite.

Transport
KTEL provide a reliable bus service between Argostóli and Skála, Póros, Kateliós, Fiskárdo, Ag Efimía and Sámi. Unfortunately, the service is limited to only about two buses a day in each direction, except for Ag Efimía which has just one bus per day.

Outside Argostóli, there *are* other services, for example between Ag Efimía and Sámi. The full bus timetable can be checked on-line at www.ktelkefalonias.gr, and timetables are available in bus stations and tourist offices. Bus fares are inexpensive.

Taxis are widely available in Argostóli and most other tourist centres. When three or four people are sharing, they can be reasonably cheap and a more convenient option than the bus. Most taxi drivers speak English, so you should be able to establish the fare before setting out or make sure the journey is being metered.

Shopping for self-catering

Most self-catering accommodation on Kefaloniá is limited to facilities for throwing breakfast together. There are usually two hot plates combined with a fridge unit, and cooking utensils are minimal. There was a time when we calculated that it was better value to eat out than buy food to cook yourself. It may not hold true now.

Few people want to waste warm evenings cooking when they could be out enjoying the atmosphere. But one or two meals can be assembled quickly without toiling in the heat. Salads are easy enough to put together, and most supermarkets have a **vegetable** section. Larger supermarkets offer a better choice of fresh vegetables — as do the local

Supermarket shopping list
washing-up liquid
washing powder for hand washing (look for the hand wash logo on the box and the word *χέρι*, the Greek word for 'hand')
olive oil soap (excellent for removing stubborn stains when hand washing)
soap
paper towels and/or napkins
aluminium foil
tissues/toilet paper
scouring pads
salt & pepper
herbs & spices
mineral water
milk
coffee/tea/drinking chocolate
butter
sugar
bread
juice
wine/beer/oúzo
sunflower oil (cooking)
olive oil (salads) & vinegar
eggs
tomato purée
rice/pasta
mayonnaise/mustard/sauces

outdoor markets. Lettuce, tomatoes, onions, cucumbers and peppers are basics which most supermarkets stock. Remember these are often **local produce** and are *not treated or sprayed* in any way to make them look or stay fresh, so they may look a little sad towards the end of the day.

Freshly barbecued chicken is also available daily and always a good start for a basic meal. Some of the dips, like *tzatzíki* and *taramasaláta,* can be bought ready-made but, to make your own *tzatzíki,* head for the **delicatessen** counter and buy the strained yoghurt *(filtráro yiaoúrti)* found in a large white plastic drum. Ask for it by weight: we find a half kilo *(misó kiló)* more than enough for two, and it's packed in a plastic container for you. This is the really thick strained yoghurt used by the tavernas to make their own *tzatzíki,* and it is also ideal for yoghurt and honey. (When making any of our recipes back home, Total yoghurt, made in Greece, is the one to use.)

The delicatessen counter is where you can buy your **cheese**, too, and there is a much larger selection than just *féta.* Avoid *féta* which has been left on display and allowed to dry out. It loses texture and becomes strongly flavoured. Always buy your *féta* from the drum where it has been kept moist under brine — or moist-looking vacuum-packed *féta.* There are a number of hard cheeses to choose from, including *kefalotíri,* well worth trying, and *kaserí.* Soft cheeses are *féta* (also available from Total in the UK) and *myzíthra.* Greeks love their *myzíthra,* a low-fat cheese rather like a smooth cottage cheese. If you can buy it unsalted (often available in spring), it's great with honey for breakfast; the rest of the year it's usually salted.

Vegetarians, vegans and those on **dairy-free** diets should have no problem finding suitable food. Moreover gluten intolerance is now widely recognised on Kefaloniá, and many supermarkets stock a good range of **gluten-free** products.

Meat and **fish** can be bought from the big supermarkets. Except for octopus, squid, tuna and swordfish steaks, most species of fish on sale may be unfamiliar. In spring and autumn, small fish like whitebait are available, which can be dipped in flour, fried and eaten whole. Ready-cleaned fish from the freezer offers an easier option for self-catering. Small, ready-made-up *souvláki*

Vegetarian, vegan, dairy- and gluten-free recipes

The two books listed below contain straightforward recipes for those with special dietary needs. Both are worth considering if you plan to self-cater in Greece, and both are lightweight paperbacks easily packed in your luggage. They are available from www.amazon.co.uk

Greek Vegetarian Cooking by Alkmini Chaitow is a book with plenty of excellent recipes and menu suggestions. It also indicates which recipes are dairy- and/or gluten-free.

A Vegan Taste of Greece by Linda Majzlik offers plenty of recipes to sample, and a concise, comprehensive listing and description of ingredients. Equally useful for vegetarians and for those on dairy- or gluten-free diets.

(**meat on a spit**) can usually be bought from the meat counter or butchers — handy if you are staying in a complex with a communal barbecue. Similarly, the **sausage** on Kefaloniá is packed with meat and another great favourite for the barbecue. All the usual selection of chops and chicken pieces is on offer.

Fruit & veg market

Argostóli has the only large fruit and vegetable market on the island, and it's open six days a week. It's located on the harbourside and does brisk business, especially in the morning.

Just about everything can be bought here, from fruit and vegetables to olives and honey.

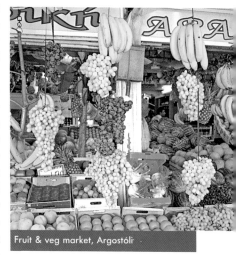
Fruit & veg market, Argostóli

Some of the vegetables may be unfamiliar, especially the greens, but they are generally named. By the way, don't expect the celery to be well blanched, it generally isn't, and there is another, unfamiliar form of celery, *célino,* which is much smaller. If you want to try your hand at cooking *hórta,* then you can buy the cultivated leaves here.

There is no fish market, but fish can be bought directly from the fishermen at the quayside in the mornings and in the supermarkets.

Argostóli, capital of the prefecture of Kefaloniá and Itháca (Itháki), spreads along the east-facing shore of an inland gulf. This circular walk around the town takes in all the major points of interest. Morning is the best time to visit; it quietens down in the afternoon, when some shops close.

argostóli

EXCURSION

Back in the 16th century Argostóli was no more than a scattering of fishermen's cottages. Building a port in this sheltered bay brought a steady increase in shipping trade and in the town's development. By 1753 it had become such an important trading centre that it was petitioning its governors in Venice to become administrative capital. In 1759, St George's Castle (see page 39) relinquished its role, and Argostóli was made capital.

It developed into a graceful town with elegant Venetian-style mansions and bell towers. Early in the 19th century it came under British

See plan inside the front cover

Grade/time: easy; allow half a day or more

Transport: 🚌 or 🚗 to Argostóli. If you arrive by bus, walk north along the front from the southern end and join the walk at the fruit and veg market. Arriving by car, the northern end of town, near the Lixoúri ferry, offers the best chance of finding a parking spot on the front. **NB:** The pay and display parking notices may not apply because of a shortage of traffic wardens. Check locally re the current situation.

Refreshments: cafés, fast-food outlets, tavernas and restaurants; see our suggestions on pages 40-41.

Opening times
Archaeological Museum: Tue-Sun from 08.30-15.00
Folklore Museum: Mon-Sat from 09.00-14.00

administration, and the first governor was the Swiss Phillipe de Bosset (1810-14), a colonel in the British Army. He brought about improvements in the island's infrastructure, including building the Drápano Bridge (see page 35) and the road over to Sámi. Colonel Sir Charles Napier, appointed governor in 1821, was just as keen to see further improvements, and more roads and public buildings followed. He created the first public park in Argostóli, Napier Gardens, which remains today, inland from the main square.

Elegance and culture ensured a good standard of living right through until the World Wars of the 20th century and the Greek Civil War which followed, when life was seriously disrupted. Just as a settled existence was returning, the 1953 earthquake (see pages 66-67) brought utter and complete devastation to the island — persuading many thousands to emigrate. Rebuilding was slow and difficult for a time but, with the help of money being sent home, grander buildings started to appear in Argostóli. Venetian-style architecture still influences present-day Argostóli, and with a large music school and theatre, its cultural aspirations remain undimmed.

Start the walk by strolling along the promenade past the **Lixoúri ferry terminal** (1). Car parking is available nearby (2). Taking the ferry over to Lixoúri is another trip to try sometime. The fare is extremely low for foot passengers, the journey time around 25 minutes, and the ferries run every 30 minutes in high season and hourly at other times. The ferry docks right in Lixoúri town, so no other transport is needed, and you can be seated at a shaded café table in the impressive main square within minutes. Alternatively, you could try Walk 2.

For now continue along the front, very shortly passing the **Greek National Tourist Office** (3); you might like to call in, if it's open. Palm trees line the now-wide promenade as the **fishing boat area** (4) is approached. This is the place to buy your fresh fish, straight off the boat. This activity always gathers interested spectators — especially the friendly logger-

Drápano Bridge

Early in the 19th century, the first governor under British administration, Philippe de Bosset, a Swiss Colonel in the British Army, announced plans to build a bridge across the Gulf of Argostóli. In those days, the head of the bay was a dangerous swamp, so boats were used to cross to the other side. Opposition to the bridge was initially strong, because many regarded their isolation as protection. But when a wooden structure 900m long was erected in just two weeks, it met with instant approval. It was eventually replaced by a stone bridge which, amazingly, was one of only a few structures to survive the earthquake. The obelisk dedicated to de Bosset part-way across gives a construction date of 1813.

With the steady increase in traffic, the bridge was threatened with closure for several years. Finally, in 2005, it was closed to traffic, but remains open to pedestrians and has recently been strengthened.

The bridge is an excellent short walk (2km return) across the bay, with the sea on one side and the lagoon which the bridge creates on the other. The yellow church at the entrance has a spectacular interior. On the far side, keep ahead along the road to the walled British cemetery on the left, with graves going back almost two centuries. You can walk beside the lagoon as well (cover photograph); the initially paved path starts by the entrance to the bridge. It soon becomes a woodland path with benches. When it ends, you can access the main road, but we prefer to retrace our steps (4km).

head turtles. The low bridge you can see crossing the gulf is **Drápano Bridge** (see previous page).

Further along are the **fruit, veg and meat markets** (6), with plenty of fresh produce on view. Most of the stalls are on the seafront side, but there are one or two opposite. Look for *hórta* among the green, leafy vegetables which are usually labelled; it's delicious and quite common on taverna menus (see page 13).

On reaching the Shell petrol station, look inland from the Shell sign to find Vas Vanderou Street, the location of one of our featured tavernas, **Tzívras** (23), a little way up on the left. Continue on the seafront only a short distance before turning

Fisherman at Argostóli

inland. (For another day: there's a lovely walkway alongside the lagoon, starting from Drápano Bridge; it makes a good short walk of 4km return.)

Cross the road, walk just two blocks up Andréa Metaxá, and turn right into pedestrianised **Lithó-stroto**. Stand by for some serious shopping. Elegant, colourful Lithóstroto is the place to be seen, and where the locals like to relax in the pavement cafés. This was the first stone-paved street on the island, as its name suggests; it's now marble-tiled, and you glide along easily. The **belltower** (8) on the left was built by the Venetians in the 18th century. Tables for cafés are set out in the small square opposite. From here you enter the world of boutiques promoting the latest fashions, brightly lit gold and silver jewellery shops, fancy goods, souvenir shops, kiosks for your instant needs and the **post office** (9). The first church encountered on the left is the Roman Catholic church of **St Nikólaos** (10) and a little further along, on the right, is the church of **Ag Spirídon** (11), Corfu's patron saint.

Venetian belltower on Lithó-stroto

Looking diagonally left at the end of Lithóstroto, you can see the Archaeological Museum (14) just across the road and, further left, just beyond the traffic lights, the **theatre** (15). Turn left and head up the street on the left of the theatre for just one block: across the road to the left is the **Folklore Museum** (16), just beside the **Korgialenos Library** (17). The museum holds a significant collection of historical items, household bric-a-brac, and costumes, giving a fairly comprehensive picture of life on the island in its heyday. There is also a collection of photographs showing pre-earthquake Kefaloniá.

Return from here back down to the **Archaeological Museum** (14): it's well organised and exhibits vases, tools, sculptures and other artefacts from the Palaeolithic to the Roman period. One whole room is devoted to the Mycenaean period which is an important part of Kefaloniá's early history (see page 104).

Continue down the street by the side of the museum and just opposite Lithóstroto. This leads past the **prefecture** (18) and the **town hall** (19) before reaching the spacious main square surrounded by cafés and restaurants. This is **Platía Valliánou**, named after the national benefactor Panayís Valliános whose statue stands in the square. The square has a great atmosphere in the evening, when the streets around are closed to traffic and alive with diners and strollers. Even with all the dining tables spread onto the square, there is still plenty of room for children to play safely in the centre.

Continue out of the square opposite to where you entered, along **Rizospastón**. The first restaurant on the left, **Arkondikó** (20), is near the **school of music** (21). Rizospastón is a wide street lined with palms and oleanders and full of elegant houses. From here you can cut down right, back to the sea front, not far from where you parked.

St George's Castle

Standing 7km southeast of Argostóli in a commanding position on a peak at 320 m, St George's Castle (free entry) is firmly woven into the history of the island. A survivor of many earthquakes, it was damaged again in the February 2014 quake, and at press date was partially cordoned off for repairs. But the views are wonderful; it is well worth a visit.

There are references to the castle as early as the 11th century, but it appears more positively in the history books in 1500, when the Turks had to defend the castle from an attack by combined Venetian and Spanish forces. In 1504 the castle was fortified to its present form, when it became the capital of the island; it remained so until 1757, when Argostóli took on the role.

Tip: 'Castro', the café by the entrance, is famous for its cheesecake!

Arkondikó

A great find for some authentic Greek cooking — a popular taverna with a homely atmosphere, friendly service and serving excellent Greek food. It's on oleander-lined Rizospastón, which is pedestrianised from the square until past the restaurant.

TAVERNA ARKONDIKÓ
Rizospastón (close to Platía Valliánou), Argostóli
all year, but on fewer days in winter €-€€

large selection of **Greek specialities**, plus **grills** and **fresh fish**; yummy *saganáki polítiko* chicken fillet
Sweets and quite a good choice of **drinks** — including different coffees, cocktails, and good **house wine**

EL GRÉCO
K Vergóti, opposite Napier Park, Argostóli
open daily all year for lunch and dinner €-€€

typical dishes include *moussaka, arakás, kokkinistó, giouvétsi,* fish and stuffed **aubergines**, etc. **Pizzas** are also available and they do a delivery service.

El Gréco

This long-established, very popular taverna has an outside enclosure at the back (open in summer). There's a lunchtime dish of the day, but an extensive menu as well. Regular visitors can request dishes to be made for the following day. And they also have a take-away service.

restaurants

eat

Tzívras

A superb find for Greco-philes in search of a really authentic Greek taverna, serving some delicious and rarely found Greek dishes.

TAVERNA TZIVRAS
Off Ioannou Metaxá, near the Shell petrol station, Argostóli
open all year at lunchtime only and some evenings €

specialities include **arakás, fakés** (recipes for both on pages 46-47), **giouvétsi** (recipe on page 135), **marídes** (small, whitebait-like fish). Their **Kefalonian meat pie** is the best we've had.

This is a taverna run mainly for Greeks at lunchtime, which is the best time to call in for a meal. It may not have an exciting location,

but it is very clean and well run. Look for Tzívras, on the left, not far along the narrow street heading inland opposite the Shell petrol station (near the fruit market on the promenade). And a bonus: they do take-away food, which you can collect and put in the fridge in your apartment for a really easy evening meal.

Old Pláka

Raised above the road, close to the marina, this taverna commands a clear view across the channel regularly plied by the Lixouri ferry. It's very popular with the locals and offers an extensive menu including several specialities.

OLD PLÁKA
Agnis Metaxá, Argostóli
open daily all year for lunch and dinner €€

a particular house **speciality** is **tsigaridia** — a mix of vegetables, herbs and spices with tomato sauce. But you can also look forward to fried **courgette keftedes** with a soft cheese & garlic dip; **pork** with prunes; **fried cheese** covered with **honey and sesame seeds** (not seen anywhere else!)

Okra is a popular vegetable in Greece, not usually available in most super markets in the UK — but it can be found in areas with an Asian population. We love this! It goes especially well with chicken and is apparently beneficial in lowering cholestrol levels.

Bámies (Okra)

Soak the okra in vinegar and water for about 15 min, rinse, drain and dry. Cut off the stalk ends carefully to a cone (not as difficult as it sounds — the aim is not to cut off the top, so the seeds remain in the pod).

Heat the oil in a large pan. Soften the onion. Add the garlic, salt and pepper, chopped tomato and okra; cook briefly, stirring gently. Then cover with water and reduce to a simmer. *Do not stir while cooking, or the okra will break up.*

Allow the water to evaporate and just leave the juices, but check the liquid level during cooking. Simmer for about 20-25 min.

<u>Ingredients (for 2 people)</u>
250 g okra
1 tbsp olive oil
100 ml crushed tomatoes or
  1 large fresh skinned and
  finely chopped tomato
1 small onion, finely chopped
1 garlic clove, crushed
salt & black pepper
water to cover

recipes

eat

Kotópoulo lemonáto me patátes (Chicken and lemon with potatoes)

Cut excess fat off the chicken legs, but leave the skin on. Mix the marinade ingredients together. Place the chicken in a container and coat all over with the marinade. Cover and leave in the fridge for a couple of hours or over-night.

Pre-heat the oven to 170°C. To cook, place the chicken legs in a roasting tin with the potatoes. Pour over the marinade and the chicken stock, to almost cover the potatoes. If there is stock left over, save for later in case the liquid requires topping up.

Cover loosely with foil, but remove the foil about half way through the cooking time. Bake for about 1 h 30 min. To keep the chicken moist, baste occsionally.

Serve with a little of the juice spooned over the chicken and vegetables of choice.

Ingredients (for 2 people)

2 chicken legs
2 medium or large potatoes, cut into chunks
250 ml chicken stock

Marinade

50 ml olive oil
50 ml lemon juice
1 level tbsp dried oregano
2 tbsp fresh parsley, finely chopped (retain a little to sprinkle over the finished dish)
2 garlic cloves, crushed
salt & black pepper

RECIPES FROM ARKONDIKÓ

Riganáda (not illustrated)

This is a speciality on Kefaloniá and is part of the starters menu.

Drizzle a little olive oil over the toast; add a sprinkling of oregano. Scatter over some tomato and *fetá* cheese. Top with black pepper, a little more oregano and a scant drizzle of olive oil.

Warm up under the grill or on a barbecue and serve immediately with a sprinkling of balsamic vinegar and chopped fresh parsley.

Ingredients (for 2 people)
2 slices of bread, dampened
   with a little water and
   toasted under the grill or on
   a barbecue
2 tomatoes, finely chopped
25 g *fetá* cheese, crumbled
dried oregano
olive oil
black pepper
balsamic vinegar
parsley (fresh), chopped

Arkondikó saláta

Arkondikó's speciality salad is a mix of rocket, shredded lettuce, pieces of cucumber and tomato tossed in a little salt and black pepper and olive oil. Pile on a plate and decorate with pieces of grilled haloúmi cheese, cherry tomatoes and a sprinkling of pine nuts. Quantity depends on the number of servings.

recipes

eat

Be aware that *exohikó (exoticó)* comes in many forms in Greece, this is just one of them. Use boned shoulder or very lean pork belly, which can be rolled, for larger numbers. Increase the stuffing accordingly and adjust the cooking time.

Exohikó (Stuffed belly of pork) *not illustrated*

Pre-heat the oven to 180°C. Mix the stuffing ingredients together.

Place the pork, flat, in a roasting tin, then secure the edges with cocktail sticks or small skewers, leaving a hole in the centre for the stuffing. Place the stuffing in the centre of the pork and press in firmly. (If using one large piece of pork, you may find it easier to lay it flat in the tin, spread the stuffing over, then roll and secure with skewers or string. Slice it before serving.)

Pour over the red wine (if using). Cover loosely with foil initially, but remove this about halfway through the cooking. Roast for about 45 min-1 h (or until the pork is tender).

Serve with mashed potatoes and green vegetables.

Ingredients (for 2 people)
2 x thick lean pieces of pork belly, about 2 cm thick; trim off excess inner fat where possible
50 ml red wine (optional)

Stuffing
25 g *fetá* cheese, crumbled
1/2 pepper (any colour), finely chopped
4 pieces sundried tomato, cut into smaller pieces

Daughter Margarita and Mum Irene of Arkondikó with Eileen

LOVE

Arakás (Peas)

This is one of our favourite dishes but not widely available in tourist areas. It's good as a shared starter or as part of a meal.

Shell the peas if you are using fresh ones, and cook the peas in some boiling water.

Heat the oil in a large pan and soften the carrot and onion. Add the other ingredients and bring to the boil, then simmer gently for 10 min.

When the carrots are soft, add the peas and simmer for a further 10 min.

Arakás: Ingredients (for 4 people)
500 g frozen peas or 1 kg fresh peas
50 ml olive oil (or 50 g butter)
1 large onion, grated
3 garlic cloves, crushed
1 tin plum tomatoes, drained and chopped, or 3 large tomatoes, skinned & chopped
1 medium carrot, finely sliced
2 tbsp fresh dill weed, finely chopped
salt & black pepper
optional: small pieces of potato can also be added

Fakés: Ingredients (for 2 people)
250 g Puy lentils, rinsed (the no-soak variety)
250 g passata or sieved tomatoes
400 ml stock made with a chicken stock cube
1 small onion, grated
1 garlic clove, crushed
50 ml olive oil
1 bay leaf
salt & black pepper
red wine vinegar to serve (optional)

recipes

eat

Fakés (Lentil soup) *ingredients opposite*

Put everything except the oil and lentils in a large pan. Bring to the boil; add the lentils and olive oil; simmer until the lentils are soft (about 30 min). Season; serve with a little red wine vinegar if you like the tang. Liquidise for a smooth texture.

Garídes saganáki (Prawn *saganáki*)

This dish is named for the cooking vessel used in Greece — a *saganáki*. Christos at Stó Psitó (see page 52) suggested adding a little gouda to help bind the ingredients when cooked.

Ingredients (for 2 people)
8 frozen king prawns, peeled and de-veined or 200 g peeled prawns or shrimps
100 ml chopped, skinned tomatoes (1 fresh tomato or tinned)
50 g *féta* cheese, cubed
1 small piece of gouda cheese, grated
1 tbsp olive oil
1 clove garlic, crushed
1 small onion, finely chopped
1 heaped tsp fresh parsley, finely chopped
1 green pepper, thinly sliced
100 ml white wine
salt & black pepper
paprika to taste

Pre-heat the oven to 170°C. Soften the onion, until it's lightly coloured, and the pepper in the olive oil. Add the parsley, garlic, tomatoes and seasoning and mix together (if using fresh tomato, cook a little to soften and reduce the moisture content). Then add the wine.

Reduce the liquid still further, then add the prawns or shrimps. Mix briefly and transfer to a shallow buttered dish. Spread the cubes of *féta* and grated gouda over the top, then some paprika to taste. Bake until the cheese is melted and bubbling (allow 5-15 min — the small shrimps will need less cooking time).

A popular walk — especially for visitors staying in Lássi or Argostóli — which follows the old carriageway along the coastline of the peninsula. The walk passes poignant reminders of the massacre of Italian troops during World War Two, but ever-changing views and refreshment options en route make for a delightful stroll.

along the piccolo yiro
WALK

Start the walk along the shore-side road in **Lássi** (**❶**), by the supermarket next to the access to Gradákia Beach; this is the start of the **Piccolo Yiro**, the old carriageway between Lássi and Argostóli. You pass **Stó Psitó** (page 52); just past it is a track left to Kalámia Beach (**6min**). The rural road winds gently downhill past an old Venetian era estate and then Oskar's on the right (**❷**; **20min**). (On the return, you will come back past Oskar's.)

You come to a long beige wall on the left with an arched gateway (**27min**). As the wall seems to end, turn left on a rough track, still skirting the wall on the left. Reaching the coast, follow the path to the right. As you pass a pleasant beach, do *not* follow the track off right: stay left, then go right, to continue along the coast. The path leads back to the road, where you turn left to the lighthouse — or first turn right for 300m to the 'Pit' (**ⓐ**), the site of the 1943 execution referred to overleaf.

Ag Theódori Lighthouse (**❸**; see page 55) was converted from a windmill during the British occupation in 1829 and rebuilt

Distance: 9.5km/6mi; 3h20min

Grade: easy walk along country roads, tracks and paths, with an ascent of 50m on the return. Take care along the road as it's used by traffic, but there is 2.3km of footpath.

Equipment: trainers or walking sandals are fine — boots if you prefer

Transport: 🚌 or 🚗 private transport to the Gradákia Beach access road at the edge of Lássi

Refreshments en route:
Stó Psitó (at the start)
Ta Didimákia at Fanári Beach
Vináries, a little under halfway along
Old Pláka (at Argostóli Marina; see page 41)

Points of interest:
Pit and memorial to massacred Italian soldiers
Ag Theódori lighthouse
Ag Theódori church
Katavóthres, a one-time corn mill
Thalassómilos, a sea mill

after the 1953 earthquake. It's a pleasant place to sit and enjoy the views and sunsets. Now the road bends right, past the small **church of Ag Theódori** on the left, to reach **Fanári Beach** and **Ta Didimákia** taverna. Soon you come to **Katavóthres** (④; see opposite). All that remains of the mill is the water-wheel and channels. Leave the road now, to follow the shady shore-side path, soon passing a track off right: it rises to the Italian Memorial visited on the return. A little further along you pass another mill, **Thalassómilos** (⑤; 'Sea Mill'), once a winery.

Continue along the shore past **Vináries** taverna (page 52), until you reach a **crossroads** (⑥; **1h40min**), where you will later continue along the road uphill on the right. For the moment, turn left downhill along Agnis Metaxá, past the **marina** and **Old Plaka** taverna on the right (page 41), as far as the **Lixoúri Ferry** departure point (ⓑ). Or carry on to the promenade at Argostóli, where you may see loggerhead turtles (especially in the morning) swimming close to returning fishing boats).

Katavóthres ('Swallow Holes')

There is a curious geological phenomenon at Katavóthres, where sea water pours into a hole in the ground. It pours down with so much force that, back in the 19th century, an Englishman built a watermill to harness the energy. Where the water disappeared to remained a mystery until a team of Austrian geologists added 160 kg of a marker dye. They discovered that the water took an easterly subterranean route to emerge partly in Melissána Cave and partly in the springs at Karavómilos on the coast (see page 106).

Following the earthquake, much less water is swallowed now at Katavóthres, and the building there, shown on page 48, has become an upmarket restaurant and nightclub.

Then return to the crossroads at the 1h40min-point and keep ahead uphill. The road bends right as it rises. You will reach the top of the road in around 15 minutes. The large **memorial** (❼) on the left, where the road bends right, commemorates the September 1943 massacre of 200 officers of the Italian 'Acqui' Division — an event still remembered each year on the island. Just beyond it, on the right, is a carefully tended **shrine to Ag Varvára** (St Barbara, patron saint of artillery) — a Greek memorial to the tragic events of 1943.

Facing the monument, go left on a track undulating along the spine of the peninsula. Fork right to a good **viewpoint** (❽), then return and follow the main track down to the right. Turn right at a T-junction (or refer to the plan inside the front cover to walk direct to Argostóli centre). After 250m, just past a hairpin bend to the right (❾), go steeply left down concrete, joining the coast road by **Oskar's** — or take the gently descending track straight ahead. Either way, turn left, back to **Lassi (3h20min)**.

Stó Psitó

A delightful balcony setting — especially at sunset — above Kalámia Beach. You enter the restaurant across a bridge spanning a pool stocked with fish and striped-necked terrapins. Plenty of choice — from a variety of Kefalonian dishes to some of Christos's own specialities.

With Christos at Stó Psitó

STÓ PSITÓ
above Kalámia Beach, Lássi
daily for lunch and dinner in high season, evenings only in shoulder season; weekends in winter €-€€

renowned for their **mezés** — the **tzatzíki** here is delicious!

sweets like mouth-watering walnut cake, cheesecake, tiramisu and 'ekmek' cake

children's menu

Vináries

This taverna/restaurant has a lovely outside area beneath pine trees, by the shore of the lagoon.

VINÁRIES
0.5km north of Argostóli marina
daily for lunch and dinner in season €-€€

Named for the wineries which once lined the shore beside the lagoon, this taverna has an extensive menu, ideal for an **oúzo and mezé** break

Lovers of seafood might like to try the **seafood spaghetti** or **seafood pilaf**

restaurants

eat

RECIPES FROM STÓ PSITÓ

The versatile dish below can include whatever mix takes your fancy — a great starter for four, or serve as a main vegetable. It can be made the day before, as it is served cold.

Lakaniká Psitá
(Roasted vegetables)

Pre-heat the oven to 160°C. Toss all the ingredients, except the balsamic vinegar, in a bowl, then place in a shallow roasting tin. Roast for about 30 min. The vegetables should be softened but not shrivelled.

Place in a dish to cool. To serve, place on individual serving dishes and drizzle over the balsamic vinegar. Decorate with pieces of fresh parsley.

Delicious served with *tzatzíki* (see recipe page 70) and olive oil bread (see recipe page 99).

Ingredients (for 4 people)
3 large mushrooms, quartered
3 peppers, cut into quarters
2 aubergines, cut into large chunks
3 medium or 2 large courgettes, cut into chunks (optional)
2-3 cloves of garlic, finely chopped
1 tbsp olive oil
salt & pepper
sprinkling of dried rosemary and oregano
balsamic vinegar

recipes

eat

53

Kotópoulo Agriliá (Chicken Agriliá)

In a large pan, soften the peppers in the olive oil, then add the pesto, sun-dried tomatoes, *féta* and olives and heat gently. When the pesto mix is blended, add the chicken pieces and heat through. Add more pesto sauce and olive oil if required.

Meanwhile prepare the rice: heat the olive oil in a pan and soften the pepper, garlic and onion. Then add the rice, pepper, cumin and stock. Cover and simmer gently for 20-30 min (brown rice will require longer). Check the liquid after 15 min and add more water if needed. The rice can of course be plainly cooked in salt water if preferred. For a special occasion, mould the rice in a small bowl and tip onto the plate to serve, as shown here.

Spoon the chicken onto a dish and serve with the rice. Decorate with a whole olive and a scattering of fresh parsley. Can be served with a salad or green vegetables such as peas or broccoli.

Ingredients (for 4 people)

300 g cooked chicken, torn into bite-size pieces
200 g jar of pesto
4 sun-dried tomatoes, or more, cut in half
100 g *féta* cheese
2 peppers, red/yellow, thinly sliced
10 black olives, stoned and cut in half. Save 4 whole stoned olives for decoration.
25 ml olive oil
fresh dill & parsley

Savoury rice

200 g rice — white, wild or brown
500 ml chicken stock (2 stock cubes)
1/2 pepper, finely diced
1 garlic clove, finely chopped
1 small onion, finely chopped
pepper (there is enough salt in the stock cubes)
1 tsp cumin
1 tbsp olive oil

Saláta koupoúra (Gardener's salad)

An ideal salad for vegetarians and vegans, this colourful mix can be adapted for non-vegans by adding chopped boiled egg, crumbly cheese or even flaked tinned tuna to make a heartier dish.

It can be served as one large salad, individually, or as a starter — adjust the quantities accordingly.

Arrange the ingredients as shown here, then pour over the dressing (perhaps adding chopped black olives as well as the corn kernels).

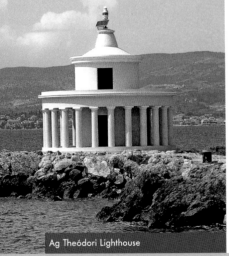

Ag Theódori Lighthouse

Ingredients (for 4 people)
1 green and 1 rosso lettuce, finely shredded
1 yellow and 1 red pepper, finely sliced
2-3 tomatoes, chopped
2 small or 1/2 large cucumber, chopped
red cabbage, finely sliced (to taste)
rocket (handful)

Dressing
1 tbsp virgin olive oil
1 tbsp balsamic vinegar
corn kernels (to taste) — and chopped black olives if liked

Lixoúri is second in size to Argostóli, although it was once the larger of the two and is still a very Greek town; worth wandering around before setting off on this walk to pretty Lépeda Beach. Little remains of the ancient city state of Páli which lies just north of Lixoúri along the coast.

lixoúri and lépeda beach

WALK

Small beach passed on the way to Lépeda Beach

The walk starts immediately on leaving the ferry at **Lixoúri** (❶). Turn left along the promenade and soon notice the main square over on the right. This is the place to stop for a coffee and/or have a short wander into the town.

Continue along the promenade, passing the **Hotel Summery** on the right. You reach the **end of the promenade (15-20min)** and leave the town behind. Carry on along the road or walk on the grass behind the shore on the left. Away from high season this road is very quiet and peaceful. You pass the cemetery church of **Ag Andréas** (❷) on the right and then come to some apart-

Distance: 6km/3.5mi; 1h30min-2h

Grade: easy with a few undulations. The walk is along footpath and a road which ends at Lépeda Beach.

Equipment: sandals or trainers, sunhat, suncream, long-sleeved shirt, long trousers, water

Transport: 🚌 to Argostóli or 🚗 (park) in the car park by the ferry terminal. Then ⛴ ferry from Argostóli to Lixoúri (every half hour, on the hour and half hour in high season, otherwise half past the hour from Argostóli and on the hour from Lixoúri).

Refreshments:
Café Pero in the square at Lixoúri (one of a few places at the start of the walk)
Taverna Apolafsi off to the right about halfway along
Ta Lépeda at Lépeda Beach (open in the season) — a small café/bar serving snacks and light meals

ments, opposite which is the small beach shown in the photograph opposite.

As you rise to a high point, a road goes right to **Taverna Apolafsi**. Keep to the country road along the shore, until you come to a T-junction. Turn left downhill to **Lépeda Beach** (❸; **45min-1h**). This lovely sandy beach is good for children. There is a shower, changing cubicle, and seasonal café/bar serving light meals.

Return the same way to **Lixoúri (1h30min-2h)**.

On arriving in Lixoúri, look for the **bronze statue of the satirical poet Andreas Laskaratos** at the port (❹) and notice that he has his back turned on Argostóli. This reflects the insult the town felt when, in 1757, the capital of Kefaloniá was moved by the Venetians from St George's castle to Argostóli instead of the then-thriving Lixoúri.

Café Pero, on the north side of the main square at Lixoúri

Café Pero

Located on the right as you enter the square in Lixoúri (see photograph opposite). Quite popular, especially with older clientèle, and serves a selection of drinks and snacks, etc.

CAFÉ PERO
main square (north side), Lixoúri
open daily €

freshly squeezed **orange juice** and **speciality coffees** (served either hot or cold) are some of the choices on offer. Excellent sandwich and snack selection.

Taverna Apolafsi

This family taverna, with its very relaxed ambience, offers a view down to the sea from its elevated terrace. Traditional food cooked by the mother, Tasia.

TAVERNA APOLAFSI
halfway between Lixoúri and Lépeda Beach
open all day in season
€-€€

large choice of **Greek specialities**, like *mezé*, salads, cockerel in tomato sauce, beef in lemon sauce, grills, fish. A great menu!

restaurants

eat

Biftéki, which translates as 'beefburgers', is often found on menus. These are usually home-made, delicious and hearty, and can be grilled, barbecued or baked in the oven.

Biftéki (Beefburgers)

Mix all the ingredients together for a few minutes. The mixture should bind well but not be too sloppy, so add the egg a little at a time. Divide into four portions and shape into round, flattened patties.

Grill 3-4 min each side, barbecue 5-6 minutes each side, or bake in the oven at 180°C for 20-30 min. The centre should be cooked but still moist.

Ingredients (for 4 large servings):
500 g lean minced beef
1 medium onion, grated
1/2 tsp dried oregano
1/2 tsp dried mint
1 tsp dried parsley (or 2 tbsp of finely
   chopped fresh)
1 tbsp red wine (optional)
1 thick slice of white bread, dunked in
   cold water (squeeze out the water
   and remove the crust)
1 small egg, beaten
salt & black pepper

recipes

eat

Ksifías (Swordfish)

Wash and dry the swordfish steaks and place them in a shallow dish. Mix the marinade ingredients and pour over the fish. Make sure the steaks are well coated. Cover and leave in the fridge for a few hours or at least 30 min.

Heat the grill to medium-high. Drain the fish and grill for 5 min each side at the most. If the steaks are thin, allow less cooking time, or the fish will become dry.

Ingredients (for 2 people)
2 (150 g) swordfish steaks
  (preferably fresh)

Marinade
1 tbsp olive oil
70 ml lemon juice
25 g plain yoghurt
1/4 tsp dried dill or 1/2 tbsp
  fresh dill, chopped
1 tsp dried mint or 1 tbsp
  fresh mint, chopped
1 garlic clove, crushed
salt & black pepper

Lépeda Beach

61

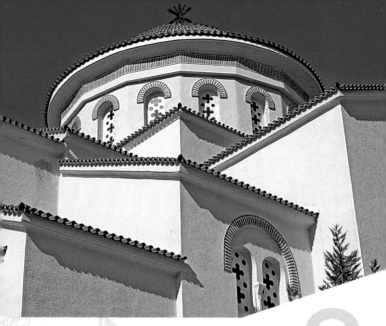

This may seem a short walk, but it will take most of the day to visit the monastery, enjoy a tasting at a nearby winery, and explore old Valsamáta — especially if you round off your outing with a meal at Bótsolos Taverna. This walk is an ideal way to experience the grape-growing plateau of the Omalá Valley.

ag gerasímos and old valsamáta

WALK

Before starting the walk, explore the monastery complex of **Ag Gerasímos** (①) by ascending the steps and heading along the left-hand side of the imposing new church. The interior decoration is impressive. Apart from Sunday services, the church is mostly open during the summer months. If the church is open, access is through the door along this side. Continue through the old archway at the end into the **convent of New Jerusalem**, founded in the 16th century by Kefaloniá's patron saint (see panel on page 65) The small church here is used during the winter for Sunday services. Leave the church through the imposing bell tower to the left.

Distance: 4km/2.5mi: 1h30min, plus time to visit the monastery and explore old Valsamáta

Grade: easy, with a climb of only 70m from the monastery to the old village of Valsamáta. A walk on a mix of country roads and tracks. *Beware, when exploring the old village, of unstable stonework and hidden holes in the ground.*

Equipment: boots or trainers (not sandals), as the track can be stony in places. Take the usual sun protection and water.

Transport: 🚌 bus or 🚗 car to Ag Gerasímos (Ag Yerasímos). Alight or park near the main steps to the new monastery. By car, turn right past the front of the steps, then park.

Refreshments en route: Plátanos (drinks only) and Bótsolos Taverna

Points of interest:
monastery complex of Ag Gerasímos abandoned village of old Valsamáta Bazigos Winery en route and nearby Robolo Winery

Once through the bell tower, **start the walk** by initially going left, then turn right uphill along the **road to Mixáta**. Around 10-15 minutes later, as the road sweeps right, stay ahead uphill on a **concrete road** (②). At the top of the rise, when you meet a crossroad/track junction, turn left. You're back on proper tarmac road almost immediately, after you walk across a **gorge** which looks like an old gravel pit. Enjoy the extensive views down left over the Omalá plain and the monastery.

Soon you reach the first ruins of **old Valsamáta**. The ruin with the pink facade (shown on the cover) was the barber's shop and possibly also served as a taverna and shop judging by its size. The walls of the **village church** (❸; **35min**) stand as a monument to the 1953 earthquake which destroyed the village in 50 seconds. Head uphill round the back of the church towards the Venetian-style base of the church tower, and notice the **cemetery** which is still in use. Further uphill, the old village street continues past a building which might have been used as an olive or wine press. The many ruins along here indicate a once-thriving community. Try not to be too tempted to explore off the main paths/tracks, as these ruins are unsafe and there may be unprotected holes. Exploring this evocative place might take some time so, when you are ready, just return to the church to continue the walk.

Stay ahead along the road past the front of the church and the smaller, more recent **chapel of Ag Paraskeví**. Ignore the concrete road downhill left, which is a shorter route to new

Ag Gerasímos

The monastery visited in the Omalá Valley is dedicated to the island's patron saint, St Gerasímos. He was born to a wealthy family in Trikala, Corinthia, and spent twelve years as a young man in the Holy Land.

Ag Gerasímos iconostasis

He settled in Zákynthos on his return, living in a cave at first, before taking holy orders there. He moved to Kefaloniá and settled in the Omalá Valley, taking over an abandoned chapel to set up a nunnery.

The rest of his life, until he died in 1579, was spent looking after the welfare of the villagers and their children. Many miracles occurred after his death, and when his body was exhumed in 1581, he was found not to have decomposed. He was declared a saint.

The small older church of Ag Gerasímos (open daily 04.00-13.00 and 17.00-21.00) was built over his tomb and the cave where he lived. The main feast days (processions, etc) are 16 August and 20 October. The saint's relics are kept in a glass case within a silver sarcophagus above the tomb.

Valsamáta (see map). You pass below and to the left of some ruins and soon you cross a narrow tarmac road. The pleasant narrow track you are on is gradually descending towards new Valsamáta. Where the track dips, five minutes/350 metres from the church, go downhill on the **concrete track** (**4**) to the left. After a few minutes, this becomes a stony track. A high wall on the left marks the boundary of small **Moní Aíyon** (**5**). Follow this round to the left and ignore a track joining from the right. Not long afterwards, stay left again, round the bend, as another

The 1953 earthquake

August 12, 1953: it took just 50 terrifying seconds to reduce the island of Kefaloniá to rubble. The fierce tremor, 7.5 on the Richter scale, ravaged Zákynthos and Kefaloniá, leaving a trail of utter destruction. Every village on Kefaloniá lost public buildings, churches and, worst of all, houses. Every village except Fiskárdo which, for some inexplicable reason, escaped relatively lightly. Some 85% of the island's housing stock was wiped out.

In the face of such devastation to roads and infrastructure, hill villages had to be abandoned in their entirety and reconstruction started again nearer the sea. The first houses built were simple, single-storey buildings, many of which still remain today. It was a decade or more before the wealth and confidence returned to build grander houses. In the face of such hopelessness, many Kefalonians left the island to seek work in America, Australia and New Zealand. It is the wealth of these returning immigrants which gives the island its present prosperity.

Two old, abandoned earthquake villages feature in our walks, old Skála and old Valsamáta. Another that you might like to explore is old

track joins from the right. On reaching a road, turn left (opposite single-storey houses). This is the edge of the **new village of Valsamáta** (⑥) which lies adjacent to the village of Frangáta on the far side.

When you reach a staggered **crossroads** (⑦; **1h06min**), keep ahead for 20m, then take the second of two roads joining from the left. You pass a cream-painted house on the right. (The main road runs parallel to this road, over to the right. By keeping ahead at the staggered junction and referring to the map, you

Fársa. It's above new Fársa, about 12km north of Argostóli. It is perhaps the most evocative of these villages to wander around and can be reached on foot in about 20-30 minutes.

Park opposite the church in Fársa and start up the narrow, very steep concrete road (also opposite the church). Follow the main route around to the left, and keep to this main track until it reaches a rise,

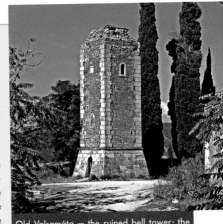

Old Valsamáta — the ruined bell tower; the ruined barber's shop is shown on the cover.

with a telegraph pole to the left and a fire hydrant on the right. At this point take the trail forking uphill to the right and continue all the way up to the ghostly, deserted village — which does, however, have a restored church.

could follow the main road to return to the start via Plátanos, Bótsolos Taverna and the Bazigos Winery.)

This pleasant route skirts two sides of the '**Field of 40 Wells**' (**8**) — three large and 37 smaller wells to aid cultivation of the valley. When the road sweeps right to the **roundabout** (**9**) on the main road with the '**Holy Well**' (which the saint purportedly dug himself), you can either follow it past the well, to Bótsolos Taverna and Bazigos or stay ahead on the minor road which zigzags back to **Ag Gerasímos** (**1h30min**).

Bótsolos

A traditional village taverna in a pleasant location, reached just before the roundabout with the Holy Well. Selection of Greek dishes, grills, etc. The menu varies daily. This place is fine for a lunch with Greek house wine.

BÓTSOLOS TAVERNA
main road, Frangáta
open all day in season €€

meze choices

Greek dishes like moussaka

fish, chicken and **meat** in various forms, and **grills**

House wine tip: White house wines in a jug are usually the best choice. If you prefer a red house wine, ask for a taste first as the red can be very variable. This is usually the case throughout Greece. Wine in a jug is sold by the kilo in Greece & we usually share half a kilo/litre — ask for a *miso kilo*.

restaurants

eat

Stifádo (Meat stew with shallots)

Lamb is the traditional meat for this dish, but beef is more widely used now. Many recipes add the shallots towards the end of cooking, but they are more tender and tastier if added from the start.

Pre-heat the oven to 170°C. Toss the meat in seasoned flour. Heat the oil in a frying pan and brown in the olive oil. Remove to a casserole dish with a slotted spoon.

Add the onions to the pan and lightly brown, then add the garlic, herbs, spices, wine and tomatoes. Bring to the boil, stirring, and pour over the meat in the casserole dish.

Cook for about 2 h, until the meat is tender. Add extra water, if needed, part-way through cooking.

Ingredients (for 4 people)
750 g lean lamb or stewing steak cut into 4 cm cubes
2 tbsp olive oil
1 tbsp flour
300 g shallots, peeled
3 garlic cloves, crushed
400 g tin of chopped tomatoes
250 ml red wine (or chicken/beef stock)
3 bay leaves
1/2 tsp cinnamon
1/2 tsp nutmeg
salt & black pepper

recipes

eat

Tzatzíki is the ubiquitous accompaniment to most Greek meals. There is often a raised eyebrow if this isn't part of your order but, of course, it's not to everyone's taste. The meat sauce for the *pastítsio* is great with spaghetti — a Greek favourite.

Tzatzíki (Yoghurt dip)
photograph on page 14

Squeeze as much liquid out of the cucumber as possible and mix well with the yoghurt. Add the garlic to taste (you may not want it too strong), a touch of olive oil, a little salt & pepper and dill if used. Garnish with olives to serve. Taste as you go!

Ingredients (for 2 people)

250 g strained yoghurt (see page 29); a medium-thick yoghurt is best, so add a drop of milk if it's too stiff

1 small cucumber, coarsely grated

2-3 garlic cloves, crushed or finely grated

olive oil

salt & pepper

fresh dill, chopped (optional)

Pastítsio (Baked meat and pasta)

Pre-heat the oven to 180°C and start by making the meat sauce. Soften the chopped onion in the olive oil, then add the meat to brown. Keep stirring until the excess liquid evaporates. Stir in the tomato paste, garlic and spice, then the remaining sauce ingredients (if using fresh herbs, add them 10 min before the end of cooking the sauce). Mix well. Leave to simmer gently for 20 min.

Meanwhile, bring a large pan of salted water to the boil and add the pasta. Reduce to a gentle boil for around 15 min, until cooked. Drain and combine with the melted butter, then the egg whites.

While the pasta is cooking, prepare the sauce. Make a roux by melting the butter in a pan. Take off the heat and blend in the flour. Heat gently to cook the flour. Remove from the heat and slowly add the milk (a whisk is useful here). Add the bay leaves, nutmeg, salt & pepper and bring to the boil to thicken, stirring constantly. Cool slightly and quickly beat in the yolks a little at a time. If the sauce is too thick, just add a little milk. It needs to be spreadable but not runny.

Grease a large lasagne-type dish and press half the pasta mix in the base. Add all the meat sauce, then the rest of the pasta. Pour over the béchamel sauce and top with either breadcrumbs or cheese. Bake for about 30 min, until the top is golden brown.

Ingredients (for 6-8 people)
750 g lean minced beef (or turkey!)
2 tbsp olive oil
1 medium onion, chopped
2 garlic cloves, crushed
150 ml white/red wine or chicken/beef
  stock
400 g tin chopped tomatoes
40 ml water
2 bay leaves
2 tsp dried parsley or 2 tbsp finely chopped
  fresh parsley
1 tsp dried mint or 1 tbsp finely chopped fresh
  mint
1 tbsp tomato paste
salt & black pepper

For the pasta
250 g penne pasta
2 egg whites, whisked
25 g melted butter

Béchamel sauce
750 ml milk
75 g plain flour
75 g butter
2 egg yolks, beaten with a fork
1/2 tsp nutmeg
2 bay leaves
salt & black pepper to taste

Topping
25 g breadcrumbs or 75 g grated
  hard cheese (*kefalotíri* is ideal if
  you are on the island)

recipes

eat

Mount Aínos (pronounced Eh-nos) may look daunting, but it is quite a friendly mountain to walk. We like to start at the park gate, but most people will shun the road and probably start at the picnic area, shortening the walk by about two hours return. Remember that it is an offence to pick or dig up wild flowers in the park.

mount aínos

WALK

Although Aínos is walker-friendly, it's subject to the vagaries of mountain weather, so be prepared — even in hot weather. We **start the walk at the gate to Mount Aínos National Park (❶)**, where there is a car park and from where it's just a matter of following the road all the way to the top.

Just before reaching the **picnic area** on the left, notice the obvious start to a path on the right via **log steps (❷**; there is a **map**). Keep heading uphill roughly in line with the road over to the left, being aware that other paths traverse the mountain and lead downhill.

When the path meets the road again, turn right to continue the short way to a **T-junction (❸)**. A right turn here leads to the the communication masts on the **summit**, but continue left along the

Distance: 14km/9mi; 5-7h

Grade: moderate-strenuous, with an ascent of just under 600m. But since it's an out-and-back route, you can turn back whenever you like. It takes around 2h45min at an easy pace (but without stops), to reach the Aínos viewpoint

Equipment: hiking boots, water *(at least 1 litre in warm weather)* and the usual sun protection. Early and late in the season take a warm lightweight top plus waterproofs, as cloud can gather around the summit.

Transport: 🚕 taxi or car as far as the gate to the national park (plenty of space to park) or the picnic area about 3km uphill (limited parking by the roadside). If using a taxi, make sure you book your return in advance.

Refreshments: none en route. The nearest tavernas are in Valsamáta (see page 68), Sámi (see page 105) and Karavómilos (see page 76).

Points of interest
spring and autumn wild flowers
endemic species of fir *(Abies cephalonica)*; it was decimated over the millennia by use for ship-building but is now protected
magnificent views

track and after 500m fork right (④) to a **high point** (1627m; ⑤; about **2h45min**). From here you have extensive views over the southeast of the island.

Return the same way to the **park gate (5-7h)**.

On the online Update for the book you can read about a hillwalker's 10-hour hike across Mount Ainos ... if you are feeling energetic!

Taverna in Karavómilos, with the original water wheel

Karavómilos Taverna

This taverna sits beside the shore of Karavómilos Lake, in company with the original, but now defunct water wheel (see photograph on page 74). The lake is fed by the waters of the Melissána Cave (see panel on page 106). There's a very pleasant outside patio area under tamarisk trees, with views towards Sámi. Plenty of traditional Greek dishes, including fish.

> **KARAVÓMILOS**
> **Karavómilos Lake**
> **daily in season** €-€€
>
> plenty of choice; Greek traditional dishes and fish — perhaps **gópes** (oven-baked small fish); **briam**, a dish similar to ratatouille

Fasolákia (Green beans)

Soften the onion and garlic in the olive oil, then add the tomato, salt and pepper and beans.

Just cover with water and boil gently to cook the beans and reduce the water (this will take approximately 25 min).

Add a drop more water if necessary, but the finished dish should have had all the excess water driven off.

Fasolákia Ingredients (for 2 people)
250 g runner beans, sliced
1 tbsp olive oil
100 ml chopped tomato, or 1 large tomato, skinned & chopped
1 small onion, finely chopped
1 garlic clove, finely chopped
salt & black pepper

restaurants

eat

Bekrí mezé (Drinkers' appetizer)

Traditionally cubes of pork in wine are used for this dish, served as a *mezé* or as a main course if cooked in a tomato sauce. You can use veal instead. There are many variations of this recipe, but this is our choice as part of a *mezé*.

This recipe needs frequent stirring throughout to stop the ingredients sticking to the pan, as minimal liquid is used in the cooking. Use a good quality meat which tenderises easily. Smaller cubes of meat will need less cooking time.

Heat olive oil in a frying pan. Sauté the onion gently, then add the meat to brown, over a gentle heat, for around 10-15 min, stirring frequently to turn the meat over.

Add the wine and continue to cook gently for a further 15 min, then add the water. Cook a further few minutes, still stirring occasionally, then add the salt and black pepper, allspice and oregano. Stir the ingredients for a further couple of minutes as there should be very little liquid left.

Serve sprinkled with fresh parsley as part of a *mezé* starter.

Ingredients (for 4 people)
300 g pork, cut into 4 cm cubes
50 ml olive oil
1 onion, chopped
100 ml red or white wine
60 ml water
1 red pepper or pieces of red/yellow/green peppers, finely sliced
1/2 tsp ground *bakhari* (allspice)
1/2 tsp dried oregano
salt & pepper

recipes

eat

An idyllic and atmospheric village, Ássos nestles in a sheltered bay (see also cover photograph) beneath the ramparts of an imposing Venetian castle connected by a thread to the mainland. A great place to unwind, explore the enchanting alleyways and absorb the ambience.

the venetian castle at ássos

WALK

Most visitors toil their way up to the castle along the winding road, but the old footpath we follow has a touch of adventure and romance.

The walk begins in **Ássos** at the start of the road leading to the castle, by the **isthmus car park** (❶). Ignore the first path uphill into the woods on the left, but take the *second* path, just beyond a **fire hydrant** (❷). This rises quite steeply at first, but soon eases out. In around **10-15min**, just past another **fire hydrant** on the right, you meet the curve of a rough track. This service track comes steeply uphill from the bend in the main track below on your right. Join this track briefly to continue uphill but, almost immediately, rejoin the path on the left.

Distance: 4km/2.5mi; 1h45min

Grade: easy, with an initial short sharp climb, then gradual uphill pull to 120m at the highest point of the walk. The path is slightly exposed on one short section, which may affect those who suffer badly from vertigo.

Equipment: boots or walking shoes, sun protection, water; jumper and waterproof in early/late season

Transport: 🚗 car or taxi to Ássos. Parking is on the isthmus or the outer loop road.

Refreshments: Tavernas Plátanos and Estiatório Mólos at Ássos, but there are other good tavernas as well, according to reports

Points of interest: the castle and Ássos village itself

The path now gently traverses the side of the slope, especially aromatic in spring, with views to an unbelievably turquoise blue sea below. A final curve uphill leads to a back **entrance gateway into Ássos Castle** (❸; **30min**). Stay ahead to reach the main cobbled track inside the castle walls.

A left turn here leads to an EU-funded complex still standing empty; it may eventually house a museum, but was damaged in

79

the 2014 earthquake. The cobbled track/path wanders north past these buildings.

To head for the main entrance, go right to continue uphill. In more recent times, the castle was used as a prison which worked a thriving agricultural enterprise within the castle walls. It's interesting to wander along, imagining the history contained among the ruins and surrounding foliage. The paved track leads to and beyond the main gateway, which was built in a dog-leg style to make access difficult for invaders.

All that is left to do now is to stroll back down the paved road, enjoying panoramic views of Ássos, back to the **car park (1h45min)**.

Footpath approach to Ássos Castle

Plátanos Taverna

A delightful taverna in the hub of the village with an amazing menu. A huge variety of Greek dishes from which to choose.

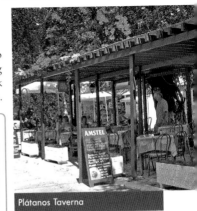

Plátanos Taverna

> ### PLÁTANOS
> **Ássos, daily in season €-€€**
>
> the **vegetarian menu** (*diáfora*) includes such mysterious names as 'gypsy food', *stifádo* with rice instead of meat; *anginarokoúkia* (artichokes with peas and aromatic herbs); *gigántes* (giant butter beans); vegetable moussaka, etc.
>
> **sweets** include a gooey chocolate pudding; *ek mek* (the Turkish name for bread), a honey brioche topped with cream; and *karithópita* (walnut cake with amaretto, recipe page 83).

> ### ESTIATÓRIO MÓLOS
> **Ássos, daily in season €-€€**
>
> the best bet here is the **fresh fish**, but there is also an extensive range of Greek specialities.

Estiatório Mólos

Estiatório Mólos

This taverna draws the crowds like a magnet because of its position at the end of the harbour on the seafront.

restaurants

eat

FROM THE MENU AT PLÁTANOS

Pikilía kreá (cold *mezé*) and *pikilía zestí* (hot *mezé*) are both found on many menus on Kefaloniá. They are particularly filling; *one portion is enough for two people* as a light meal. Below is a list of ingredients, and the picture illustrates how they are presented.

Pikilía kreá (cold mezé)

This dish makes an ideal starter or something to have with drinks and nibbles at home.

Hot *mezés* could include fried whitebait, cheese balls (both recipes in *walk & eat Rhodes*), roasted peppers (page 53), courgette balls (page 136), mini meat balls (page 128) and slices of fried sausage.

<u>Ingredients (for 2-4 people)</u>
olives
dolmádes (stuffed vine leaves)
cucumber
tomato
capers
artichokes
spicy cheese dip (page 122)
melitzána saláta (aubergine salad, recipe page 122)
tzatzíki (recipe page 70).

Both versions of the cake on the next page are also found as Kefalonian specialities, although there are a myriad of versions around Greece. The darker walnut version is the one we found mainly, but the basic recipe is the same for both. Use either almonds or walnuts — or a mix of both! I made the almond version, recipe below, and substan-

recipes

eat

tially cut down the sugar content. Greek versions usually have 12 eggs, 12 tbsp sugar, etc.

Amygthalópita or Karithópita (Almond or walnut cake)

Pre-heat the oven to 170°C. Grease and line the base of a 21 cm/8 in round spring-form tin or similar.

Separate the egg whites from the yolk. Dissolve the baking powder in the brandy. Whisk the yolks and sugar until creamy, then add the breadcrumbs, almonds/walnuts, water, cinnamon and brandy/baking powder.

Karithópita

Whisk the egg whites and fold into the nut mixture. Pour into the tin. Bake for 20 min or until a skewer inserted in the middle comes out clean.

Leave the cake in the tin and pierce holes all over the surface with the skewer. Pour over the cooled syrup while the cake is still warm, then pour over the optional amaretto. (Some recipes add the finely grated zest of half an orange or lemon — in which case substitute the juice for some of the syrup water.)

When cold, cut into slices and serve with cream or ice cream (but it's equally good served on its own). Will freeze wrapped in foil. Best served the day after it's made.

Ingredients (for 12-16 servings)
150 g ground almonds or
  walnuts
15 g breadcrumbs
40 g sugar
125 ml water
3 eggs
1/2 tsp cinnamon
1/2 tsp baking powder
12 ml brandy
30 ml amaretto (optional)

Syrup
75 g sugar
1 small cinnamon stick
3 cloves
200 ml water

There are many variations on the **mousakás** theme, but all basically contain the same ingredients. It's a matter of personal taste how you put them together. Some recipes use only aubergines; others (including ours), potato. Anything goes; it depends a great deal on the flavouring.

This is an easy recipe to adjust for any number of people. Even the topping can be a straightforward cheese sauce, béchamel, or one containing egg yolk. We use the béchamel option in this recipe, but it's worth experimenting with the different options.

Frying the aubergines and potatoes can turn this into a very oily (but very tasty) dish. But the aubergine slices can be brushed with oil and baked or dry-fried. Our long-used method is to layer the aubergine (1 cm thick slices) in a dish, drizzling a little oil over each layer: cover with clingfilm and microwave until soft, around 8-10min. Halve the potatoes and boil them until almost cooked.

Mousakás (Moussaka)

Pre-cook the aubergines and potatoes as above. Heat some oil in a frying pan and gently stir-fry the onions and garlic to soften. Add the meat and brown, still stirring. Drain off any excess fat/liquid. Now add the herbs, spices, and salt & pepper to taste. Moisten with the tomato juice if using tinned. Grease a 2.5 l ovenproof dish or large casserole.

Place a layer of aubergine slices in the base of the dish, then the meat. Top with a further layer of aubergine slices and the chopped tomatoes. Finally, place a layer of sliced potatoes on the top.

For the sauce, make a roux with the flour and butter by melting the butter and combining with the flour then, using a balloon whisk, gradually add the milk and seasoning. Continue to stir over the heat until the mixture boils and thickens. (If using a microwave, melt the butter, then add the flour using a balloon whisk to combine the two, and microwave on high for 40 seconds. Gradually whisk in the milk and seasoning. Microwave on high for 2 min, stir, then continue in

1 min bursts, stirring in between, until the sauce bubbles and thickens. Watch carefully, to prevent the mixture boiling over.)

Spread the sauce over the mixture in the dish, sprinkle over some grated cheese and bake at 180° C/gas mark 4 for 30-40 min, until brown on top.

The *mousaká* can be frozen for a few weeks or left overnight on the chiller tray in the fridge, which will enhance the flavour.

Alternative vegetarian version: Replace the meat with about 100 g of cooked puy or green lentils and a mixture of sliced vegetables. For example, heat some olive oil and butter in a frying pan, soften 2 onions, then add 2 sliced carrots, 2 sliced sticks of celery, 4 large chopped tomatoes (or a 400 g tin of tomatoes), a handful of fresh parsley, salt & pepper and an optional dash of red or white wine. Simmer for around 30 min, then add the cooked lentils. Use as the meat layer in the main dish.

Alternative topping: Use the basic sauce recipe, seasoned with salt & pepper, then stir in 1 egg yolk and 60 g of grated cheese.

Ingredients (for 6 people)

500 g lamb or beef, minced
2-3 pre-cooked aubergines (1 kilo)
2 pre-cooked medium potatoes
2 medium onions, chopped
3 garlic cloves, crushed
1 tin (400 g) plum (or chopped) tomatoes, or 4 large ripe tomatoes, skinned & chopped
1 tsp basil
1 tsp oregano
1 tsp allspice
salt & pepper to taste
olive or other oil (to drizzle over the aubergines and for frying)

For the béchamel sauce

600 ml warmed milk
2 tbsp flour
60 g butter
1/2 tsp nutmeg
2 bay leaves
ground black pepper

Picturesque Fiskárdo is at the heart of 'yachtie-land' on the island — it's fascinating to watch the comings and goings in the morning and late afternoon. This is a pleasant walk through tranquil rural countryside, still with signs of a now-lost old way of life. There's also the prospect of a good lunch at Andipáta!

circuit from fiskárdo

WALK

6

Start the walk from the **ferry quay** in **Fiskárdo** (**❶**): continue along the road by the shore, away from the village. In three minutes, leave the road and stay ahead on a path, still following the shore (waymarks: **yellow splashes** and **blue stripes on a white ground**). (Just at the outset, a left turn leads directly to the basilica.) You pass the **old Venetian lighthouse** (**❷**) on the right and walk to the right of the **new lighthouse** a minute later (ignore the path on the right to the shore here). Stay with the waymarks and soon you will see ruins ahead. Rise to the **ruined Christian basilica** (**❸**; **20min**) and keep ahead through the remains. Ahead is the lighthouse at the tip of the island of Lefkáda.

Once through the ruins, follow **yellow blobs**: ahead is a fence, and to the left private property. Follow the arrowed

Distance: 10.5km/6.6mi; 3h30min

Grade: moderate, with a few uphill sections of around 140m overall. The walk can be split quite easily into three shorter walks:
(1) to Émblissi Beach and back along the road
(2) taxi to Andipáta (To Pétrino for lunch) and walk back to Fiskárdo
(3) from Fiskárdo to Andipáta and back along the main road (just 1.7km)

Extension: the 'Battery Trail' (2014), shown on the car park information board (blue/white waymarks); *for experienced route-finders*

Equipment: sturdy walking shoes, sun protection, swimwear, jumper/waterproof in early/late season

Transport: 🚌 or 🚗 car to Fiskárdo. No traffic is allowed in the village, so park in the car park with the information board.

Refreshments: ample; we feature To Pétrino at Andipáta and Captain's Cabin and Lagoudéra in Fiskárdo

Points of interest:
two good beaches
old Venetian lighthouse
early Christian basilica
Andipáta
the abandoned village of Psilithriás
church of Ag Spiridon
Throne of the Queen of Fiskárdo

path to the right, to a gravel track. Turn left here (a villa is to your right; **④**; **35min**) and go through open gates.

The track soon becomes a concrete road (**45min**), which you follow uphill. Meeting the **main road** (where Fiskárdo is 0.7km to the left), turn right. Then, in just one minute, turn right downhill. In under four minutes, look for a path downhill through woodland on the left. This cuts out some road-walking, but is only for the agile. It emerges on a road leading to a **sub-station**. Turn right to the car park at **Émblissi Beach** (**⑤**; **1h**).

Continue through the car park behind this brilliant white-stone beach. At the far side, pick up your onward path at the right of the snack bar. The stone-edged path turns sharply left uphill in under a minute and rises gently through a fairy-tale forest of strawberry trees and holm oaks. Unfortunately the path is not always clear, so go carefully, remembering that you are walking roughly parallel with the (unseen) coastline.

Quite suddenly you arrive at **Kymiliá Beach** (**6**; **1h45min**), a great place to rest for a while. Then look for the uphill path towards the far end of the beach. Turn left off the beach, then go left almost immediately on a wide clear path marked with a **red dot**. Gradually climb inland through woodland for 15 minutes or so and, when you meet a track (**2h**), turn right.

Fiskárdo harbour

Very soon, look for a stony section of bank on the right where a wooden post, with arrow, indicates the start of a path through woodland. Follow this blue/white-waymarked path carefully. When you reach a rough, stony crossing trail, turn right. This path dips into a hollow and rises again. Then you meet a crossing forestry track (**7**; **2h20min**), where you turn left uphill (ignoring the 'Battery Trail' waymark on the right). When you come to a wire fence across the track, lift it away (on the left) and replace it. Then you arrive on the bend of another cross-track. Stay ahead uphill on this track, which becomes concreted. In around five minutes you pass Anestis House on the right and meet a road. Turn left; you will come to the main road at **Andipáta** a good five minutes later. **To Pétrino** taverna (see page 92) is just to the right here — opposite a small supermarket and café/ snack bar.

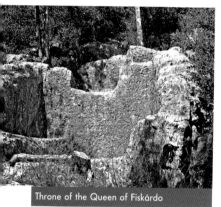

Throne of the Queen of Fiskárdo

Leave To Pétrino along the main road to the right, heading away from Fiskárdo, with Andipáta's **church** (❽) on your left. Immediately past the church, turn left on the road signposted in Greek to Psilithriás. This section of road-walking is through pleasant rural countryside. You pass the old village of **Psilithriás** over to the right — mostly abandoned since the earthquake. The old church of **Ag Spirídon** sits in an elevated position, from where Fiskárdo can be seen, but just before it's reached, fork right on a stony track (❾; **2h55min**).

In under 20 minutes, as you approach the Queen Club on the right, the **Throne of the Queen of Fiskárdo** (❿) is set back in the trees over to your left. The hollows and steps hewn out of the rock suggest that it might once have been a necropolis.

When you reach the main road at the back of **Fiskárdo**, either turn right, back to the **car park**, or cross over and walk past the excellent Tselentis Bakery on the left (they make one of the best *spanakopitas* we've ever had), to the **harbour** (**3h30min**).

Captain's Cabin

A popular and long-established taverna. situated right on the waterfront in the middle of yachting activity.

Lagoudéra

Another restaurant serving very good Greek food, but also offering a good fish selection — including lobster. And, like Captain's Cabin, it is an excellent place from which to watch the 'yachties'.

Captain's Cabin (above); Lagoudéra (below left)

CAPTAIN'S CABIN
waterfront, Fiskárdo
open all day in season €-€€
specialities: rabbit *stifádo*, Kefalonian meat pie, Captain's sea food platter (king prawns, swordfish, *kalamári*), vegetarian dishes

LAGOUDÉRA
waterfront, Fiskárdo
open all day in season €-€€
a **good Greek menu** with specials like ham and beef stew in white sauce

restaurants
eat

To Pétrino

To Pétrino — the name means 'The Old Stone House' — replaces our original recommendation in Andipáta, To Péfko. That restaurant was severely damaged in the earthquake of 2014. To Pétrino is fine and very well situated for this walk, beside the road and with a shaded recessed patio, but To Péfko was really special — and the recipes on the following pages are all from To Péfko. The proprietor, Xrisanthe, was constantly experimenting with new ideas (see pages 98-99). She now runs the supermarket opposite To Pétrino, but no longer has a taverna, alas.

Her olive oil bread was delicious! My efforts at home (see page 99) gradually worked out, with the addition of some sugar, as Greek flour may naturally contain more sugar. This bread goes well with soup and starters, but it needs to be eaten straight away or frozen. It's a case of experimenting; breads made at home tend to be more dense, but still tasty.

TO PÉTRINO
main road, Andipáta
open all day in season €-€€

extensive menu of **Greek dishes** including *piklilia* — a plate of mixed starters, ideal as a shared dish with a glass of wine

large selection of **salads**

seafood dishes, including a **seafood platter**

meat dishes like pork tenderloin in amaretto sauce

full **English breakfasts**

pasta, pizza, snacks

restaurants

eat

Pandzária (Beetroot)

This *mezé* is delicious early in the season, when the leaves are also served with the beets. Warm or cold, it goes well with *skordaliá* (see page 128). Wash thoroughly and cut off the leaves. Boil the beetroot in a large pan of boiling salted water for about 35 min (depending on size), until tender. Rinse under cold water, then peel while still warm and cut into wedges or slice. Heat the oil in a pan and stir in the leaves until they wilt. Add the cut beetroot, lemon juice and seasoning; mix well.

Ingredients (for 4 people)
1 kg fresh beetroot with leaves
2 tbsp olive oil
1 tbsp fresh lemon juice
salt & pepper

Tonnos (Tuna)

Rub the marinade mix all over the steaks and leave in the fridge for 15 min. Then grill on an oiled griddle or barbecue no more than 2-3 min each side — just to sear (otherwise tuna becomes too dry).

Tonnos: Ingredients
(for 2 people)
2 x 150 g tuna steaks, about
2 cm thick

Marinade
1 tbsp olive oil
1/2 tsp dried oregano
1/2 tsp dried thyme
salt & black pepper

recipes

eat

Kefalonian meat pie is a traditional pie of the island found in almost every taverna, but don't expect them all to be the same — there seem to be almost as many variations as days of the year.

Kefalonítiki kreatópita (Kefalonian meat pie)

Pre-heat the oven to 180°C. Heat the olive oil in a large pan, brown the meat and soften the carrot and onion. Dissolve the tomato paste

in the wine. Add the garlic, wine and tomato paste, parsley, dill and salt and pepper, and mix together well. Remove from the heat.

To prepare the pastry, mix together the flour, salt and sugar. Make a hole in the centre and pour in the oil, white wine, and half the water. Mix together to

Ingredients (for 2-3 people)

500 g lean lamb, cut into dice-size cubes
100 ml olive oil
1 onion, grated
2 garlic cloves, crushed
2 small carrots, finely sliced
1 tbsp tomato paste
150 ml white wine (or water)
20 ml water (added just before cooking the pie)
1/2 tsp ground nutmeg

1 heaped tbsp fresh parsley, finely chopped
1 heaped tbsp fresh dill, finely chopped
salt & black pepper
100 g quick cook rice

Pastry
250 g plain flour
1/2 tsp salt
1/2 tbsp sugar
40 ml olive oil
40 ml white wine

In the past the pie was made from goat, but a mix of meats can be used. Kid doesn't need pre-cooking, but the tougher older goat meat needs tenderising. Beef, pork and lamb seem to be more commonly used now. Some recipes use lentils in place of rice, and some have egg in the pastry. Herbs and spices as well are mainly dictated by personal preference, but parsley is usually found in most pies. Pre-soften the rice a little if it isn't the quick cook variety.

make a pliable dough, adding more water as needed. Knead well together.

Grease a round 20cm/8in cake tin. Line the tin with about two-thirds of the pastry (enough to line the tin and overhang the rim), then roll out the remainder to fit the top of the tin. Place the meat mixture in the tin and scatter the rice over the top to prevent the rice from sinking. Although it may appear to be quite liquid, add the 20 ml of water. Cover the pie with the pastry lid and fold over the edges. Curl the two pieces firmly together and make slits in the centre.

Place the tin in a roasting tin and bake for 1 h, until the crust is golden brown. Leave to settle a short while before serving with peas or perhaps okra.

Fasóli mavromátiko
(Black-eyed beans)

Soak the beans in water overnight, then drain. Boil gently in a large pan of water, which generously covers the beans, for about 1 h; add more water if needed. They are ready when they are soft but still firm; do not overcook, or they will become mushy.

Drain and place in a bowl. Mix all the other ingredients with the beans and serve warm or cold. Tasty alone as a vegetable mixed with some black pepper; reheats easily in the microwave.

Ingredients (for 4 people)
200 g black-eyed beans
1 garlic clove, crushed
3 tsp vinegar
25 g olive oil
some chopped fresh parsley
2-3 spring onions, chopped (or 1
   red onion, finely sliced)
salt & black pepper

recipes

Spetsofáï (Sausage and peppers in spicy sauce)

The sausage alone makes this quite a spicy dish for most tastes, but for a red-hot version replace one pepper with a hot pepper.

Soften the onions in the olive oil gently, stirring. Stir in all the other

ingredients, except the wine, until well mixed; then add the wine. Cover and cook over a gentle heat for 25-30 min, stirring from time to time.

This is usually served on its own in a clay dish, but for large appetites serve it on a bed of rice or pasta, or with mashed potatoes.

Ingredients (for 4 people)
- 400 g spicy sausage like pepperoni, sliced
- 3 large peppers, thickly sliced (usually green, but red or yellow brighten up the dish)
- 2 onions, sliced
- 1 aubergine, sliced (optional)
- 1 400 g tin chopped tomatoes
- 2 garlic cloves
- 2-3 tbsp red/white wine or water
- 2 tbsp olive oil (add more if needed)

Spetsofáï (top) and chicken curry (above)

Kotópoulo me káru (Chicken curry with rice and lemon) (photograph opposite)

Unless you prefer to cook it on the hob, pre-heat the oven to 170°C. Trim excess fat off the chicken legs. In a large pan, soften the onion, then brown the chicken legs. Mix in the garlic, and stir in the tomato paste with the wine. Boil off some of the wine, then add the tomatoes, parsley, cinnamon, nutmeg, salt and pepper. When the chicken is partially cooked, mix 1 tsp of the curry powder with half the lemon juice and pour over the chicken.

Continue cooking gently on the hob or transfer to a casserole; pour over the curry and lemon, and cook 1 h — longer if needed. In either case, baste with the juices occasionally to keep moist.

Bring the 350 ml water to a boil, add the other 1 tsp of curry powder, and boil the rice for 20-25 min (longer for brown rice). Top up the water as necessary.

Place the chicken and some juice on a plate with the rice and pour over the warmed remaining lemon juice. Good with green beans, peas or broccoli.

Ingredients (for 2 people)

2 chicken legs, skinned
60 g soft margarine or butter
100 ml white wine
1 tsp tomato paste
1 small onion, chopped
2 garlic cloves, finely chopped or crushed
2 fresh tomatoes, skinned and chopped or 1 small tin of chopped tomatoes
1 tsp dried parsley or 1 tbsp of chopped fresh parsley
1/2 tsp cinnamon
1/2 tsp nutmeg or ground cloves
2 tsp curry powder (add more for a stronger curry flavour)
75 ml lemon juice (juice of 1 lemon — warm the lemon in a microwave first to increase the juice yield)
100 g rice
350 ml water
salt & black pepper

recipes

eat

TO PÉFKO SPECIALITIES

Kléftiko ('Cooked in a parcel')

Pre-heat the oven to 180°C. Grease two large squares of aluminium foil. Brown the meat cubes in 1 tbsp of the olive oil. Add a further

1 tbsp of olive oil and soften the onion, carrot and potato, stirring. After a couple of minutes add the garlic, peas, oregano and salt and pepper. Cook for a further couple of minutes.

Divide the mixture into two equal portions and place in the middle of the foil sheets. Gather up the sides of the foil a little, to form a bowl. Scatter over the cheese, place tomato slices on the top, and sprinkle over a little more oregano.

Gather in the sides of the foil, to form a sealed parcel and place in a roasting tin. Bake for about an hour. Serve the parcels immediately, on individual plates, with extra vegetables if desired.

Ingredients (for 2 people)

300g lean lamb cut into dice-size cubes
2 tbsp olive oil
1 small onion, finely chopped
1 garlic clove, crushed
1 potato, cut into small cubes
1 carrot, thinly sliced
60 g frozen peas
2 tbsp lemon juice
1/2 tsp dried oregano
2 small or 1 medium tomato, sliced and cored
50 g *féta* or Lancashire cheese, crumbled or cubed
salt & black pepper

Péfko saláta (Pine tree salad) photograph and ingredients opposite

Toss all the ingredients in a bowl with a little olive oil and the seasoning. Arrange on a plate and drizzle over some balsamic vinegar.

recipes • kléftiko, péfko saláta, eleólatho psomí

Eleólatho psomí
(Olive oil bread)

Mix the dried yeast and sugar with some of the water to dissolve and activate the yeast, so that it becomes a thin runny paste.

Sift the flour and salt in a bowl and make a well in the centre. Pour in the olive oil and the yeast paste with most of the water and mix to a soft pliable dough, adding more water as needed. Knead well (about 10 min by hand).

Leave to rise in a warm place for 50 min-1 h (it will double in size). Knead again for a few minutes until smooth. Then divide into roughly 66 g pieces of dough and quickly roll into balls. Place these on a greased and floured baking tray and leave to rise again in a warm place, while you pre-heat the oven to 180°C,

When risen, bake 20-25 min. The bottoms should sound hollow when cooked if tapped.

Bread: Ingredients (for 12 rolls)
500 g strong white bread flour
15g dried yeast
85 ml olive oil
1/2 tsp sugar
1/2 tsp salt
250 ml lukewarm water

Pine tree salad: Ingredients (for 2 people)
100 g cooked chicken pieces (bite size)
lettuce, shredded
red cabbage, finely shredded
1 small tin kidney beans, drained and rinsed
1/2 cucumber, cubed
olive oil
salt & black pepper
balsamic vinegar

Pine tree salad: quantities of lettuce and red cabbage have been left to individual taste.

recipes

eat

Although Sámi is now a modern town and port, it must have been a sight to behold when it was a magnificent walled city, known as Kyatis. It later became an important Roman naval port before its decline. The ancient stones were used in the 13th century to build the Ag Fanéntes monastery, which existed for 600 years.

above sámi

WALK

Start the walk at **Platea Kyprou** (**❶**) in **Sámi**, opposite the **statue to seamen** on the promenade. Head inland on Odós Príamou and soon reach a small **square with a huge plane tree**. Bear slightly left, but stay ahead, to the left of the tree. (A few hundred metres along the road to the left here leads to the remains of Roman baths on the right.) Rise to a T-junction, with a **church** on the left-hand corner, and turn left. In a further minute leave the road, just before reaching a **wall with iron railing**s, by turning sharp right uphill on a path

> **Distance:** 5.5km/3.4mi: 2h
>
> **Grade:** easy-moderate, with a climb of around 280m/924ft, or more if you explore the acropolis hill. A fairly gradual ascent, with a steep descent from Ag Fanéntes. For a shorter walk go directly to Ag Fanéntes from the 20min-point and retrace your steps.
>
> **Equipment:** hiking boots, water, sun protection, warm top/waterproof in early/late season
>
> **Transport:** 🚐 (check timetable locally), 🚕 taxi or car to Sámi centre
>
> **Refreshments:** none en route, but plenty in Sámi, including two featured tavernas — Mermaid and Deco
>
> **Points of interest:** the two acropolis hills of Ag Fanéntes and Paleókastro (the larger of the two) overlooking Sámi; both were part of ancient Sámi

marked with a **red dot** and a **walkers' information board** (**❷**). Then turn sharp left uphill a minute later. In another minute, at a **clearing with pine trees** and the remains of some ancient walls, keep left uphill on the main path. A small **retaining wall** jutting out into the path (**❸**; **20min**) marks the point where the return route emerges from Ag Fanéntes (*turn right here for the shorter walk*).

Stay ahead to continue climbing alongside the valley separating the two hills, initially through woodland. In a few minutes, notice the part-buried remnants of what was possibly a sarcophagus on the right and another a little further along. When you emerge into the open, you will see the remains of the acropolis on the hill across the valley on the left. The path starts to swing more to the left across the head of the valley. Once at the base of the hill, keep uphill to the right, still following occasional waymarks, to emerge on a flat area.

To continue uphill, bear diagonally left and rise over terraces into a goats' field, with the acropolis of **Paleókastro** over to

Captain Correlli's Mandolin

There was a Kefaloniá loved by many before Louis de Bernières' best-selling book, but there is no doubt that both the book and the subsequent film boosted tourism to the island.

Filming the book on Kefaloniá created problems, since the action is set during World War Two, in a pre-earthquake Argostóli. Just a minor hurdle for the film industry — they simply reconstructed a replica of old Argostóli in Sámi and of another village on top of the hill between Sámi and Antísamos.

The locals wanted to preserve the stage set, but the story extends into the earthquake period — so the stage set, like Argostóli, crumbled and collapsed. All that remains now is a noticeboard at the beginning of the track at Dikália showing pictures of the stage set.

your left. Keep right along the edge of the field, to the fence and road.* To get to the road, climb the bank on the right and skirt round the end of the fence.

Go right on the **road** (**4**; under **1h**) and soon pass a waymarked path downhill to Antísamos Beach on the left, about 30-40min away. Enjoy elevated views of the acropolis walls and then over Sámi harbour. From the extensive ruins of **Ag Fanéntes** (**5**) the road descends left downhill, to the main road. But keep ahead; your onward route is at the far side of the ruins.

To continue, go down the steps to the left of the bell opposite the entrance to **Ag**

Bell at Ag Nikólaos

*But to explore the acropolis, or as another way to get to the road, stay left along the back edge of the field. Rise gently left onto the next terrace and stay ahead between a huge olive tree down to the right and the hill. When you reach a rough, rising track, follow it to the left uphill to explore further, or go briefly left, then right on a path which leads back to the road. Add 10min/0.6km.)

The Mycenaean cities (1400-1100BC)

There is clear evidence of a well-organised Mycenaean civilisation on both Kefaloniá and Itháca. Major settlements were spread around Kefaloniá at Sámi, Páli, near Lixoúri, Próni, between Skála and Póros, and at Kráni, near Argostóli.

Since the Mycenaeans built with massive stone blocks, remains of their cities are still visible. Kráni, located between Argostóli and Sámi, is one of the best examples. Head towards Sámi: 3.3km after leaving the side of the lagoon, just after the sign for Razata village, look for a narrow road off right with a large red-roofed shrine at the entrance. On the wall, just as you turn into the road, is a large sign to Kráni. The road eventually becomes a track and leads to the site. Walkways have been cleared around the site, which makes it much easier to get about, and you can explore the very extensive Cyclopean walls shown here. The extent of these walls can best be seen on Google Earth.

Nikólaos church (usually locked). This newer church has replaced a ruined 17th-century church sited below. Stones line the route of the onward path, but first divert left to locate the path down to the **ruined Ag Nikólaos church with frescoes** (**⑥**).

Then return to the stone-lined path and follow this down the terrace and then to the right. Head across a bed of pine needles and stay on the path as it winds fairly steeply downhill. Bay trees grow in abundance on the hillside here, so cooks could collect a few leaves to take home on the way down. In 20 minutes or so you meet a crossing path (your outward route); turn left and follow it down to **Sámi** (under **2h**).

Mermaid Taverna

A busy taverna located on the quayside in Sámi. A pleasant place to enjoy a leisurely lunch.

MERMAID TAVERNA
Sámi seafront
open all year, but less often in winter €-€€

specialities include rabbit *stifado* and 'chicken Mermaid' — rolled and boned chicken with ham and cheese filling, served with a mustard and 'secret ingredient' sauce

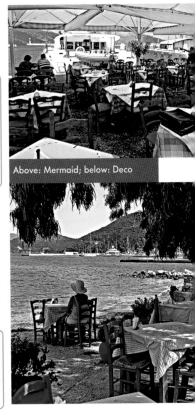

Above: Mermaid; below: Deco

Deco

Left from the square in Sámi, on the inland side of the road, but with some tables on the beach. (It is next door to Il Familia, which you pass first when coming from the square — another good restaurant.)

DECO
Sámi seafront (inland side)
only open in the season €-€€

large selection of **kefalonian specialities**; the owner, George, was once a butcher in Argostóli

restaurants

eat

Melissána and Drogaráti caves

With an island which is virtually a great mass of limestone, it is not surprising to find caves. These two have been organised and commercialised.

Melissána, located not far from Karavómilos, has a collapsed roof and is filled by a lake. A tour of this cave means a 10-minute trip in a rowing boat. An oarsman rows steadily across the lake into a far channel and back again. Legend has it that in ancient times huge stalactites made of pure honeycomb hung in the cave, hence the name (*melissá* means honeybee).

Drogaráti Cave, south of Sámi and Karavómilos, is visited on foot. More than 100 steps lead down to a platform for the first view of stalactites and stalagmites within an illuminated cavern. Further steps lead down to a walkway circling the lowest cavern which is sometimes used to host concerts. The wet rock and steps can be slippery underfoot, so wear suitable shoes, *not* sandals.

Exploring the Melissána (left) and Drogaráti caves (below)

Kalamári tiganitó (Fried squid)

Use fresh or frozen squid. Clean if necessary, then dry thoroughly. The tentacles will be separate, but leave small squid *(kalamárakia)* whole and cut large fish into rings.

All that is needed is to coat the squid with peppered flour and fry in hot fat for about 3 min, until brown and crispy. *Overcooking toughens the flesh.* Drain on kitchen paper. Serve with lemon.

Kolokithákia tiganitá (Battered courgettes)

This dish is great as part of a *mezé* or to serve with drinks. Beat the batter ingredients well, adding enough water to make the batter thick enough to coat the courgettes thinly.

Heat a 2 cm depth of olive/rape seed oil in a frying pan until a drop of batter sizzles. Dip the courgette slices in the batter, shaking off any excess. Fry in the hot oil for a minute, then turn over for a further minute or until golden brown. Remove with a slotted spoon and drain on kitchen paper before serving.

Ingredients (for 4 people)
500 g courgettes, sliced in thin rings

Batter
150 g plain flour
1/2 tsp baking powder
1 tsp vinegar
salt & black pepper
water

recipes

The seas around Kefaloniá are the deepest blue, deeper than we can recall anywhere else in the Mediterranean. It fits Homer's descriptive 'wine-dark sea' so perfectly. This excursion sails across the wine-dark sea to the nearby island of Itháca, legendary home of Homer's great hero, Odysseus.

over the sea to itháca

EXCURSION

Mountainous Itháca (Itháki) is virtually two islands, joined by a narrow neck of land. Píso Aetós, where the ferry docks, lies on this narrow neck, so this car tour first circles the northern part of the island (where there's more to see), then returns south to Vathí.

Follow the road which winds up from **Píso Aetós** to a saddle where the ancient **Mycenaean site of Alalka-menós** is located on the left. It's an open site, so you can wander along marked routes to inspect the giant walls and entrances — but this is best left till the end of the day, when you can fill in time waiting for the return ferry. Within minutes you are descending towards the coast on the far side of the neck and the junction with the main road. Turn left here and head north along the coast road — but not for long, since the road

Description: a full day out, with a 45min ferry ride each way and over 6h to explore Itháca; **see map on page 110**

Transport: ferry from Sámi, Póros or Fiskárdo. The Póros ferry is a major line and much more expensive; ferries from Fiskárdo only run in high season. The Sámi ferry is the most regular and reliable: it departs at 08.45; tickets can be bought on the day at the shipping agent on the front, and the crossing takes about 45 minutes. The last ferry back departs at 16.30, which leaves plenty of time for a complete tour of the island (some 70km of driving). There is no point in crossing without a hire car, since the ferry docks on Itháca at Píso Aetós which is about 8km outside the main town of Vathí, and there is no public transport. It's important to mention your intention to ferry across to Itháca when you hire your car, to make sure the insurance covers this option.

Refreshments: There is plenty of choice of tavernas, and most serve the locals, so finding lunch should be no problem. We haven't featured any particular places on this excursion, since it depends on where you happen to be at lunch time.

soon leads back over the narrow neck towards the other coast. As you rise away from the coast, take the right turn to Anogí and climb more steeply for a time. Notice, shortly, the road off left to **Moní Katharón**. Dedicated to Panayía Kathariótissa, this monastery is the religious centre of the island. Although devastated by the 1953 earthquake, it was completely rebuilt. The height at this point is 556m, so the views from the monastery — or anywhere on this section of the road, looking down over the highly sculptured and indented coastline around Vathí — are breathtaking.

This high-level route soon leads to **Anogí**, the highest village on the island (520m). Once the island's main town, it's now very sleepy, although there is a café/bar. The eye-catching Venetian campanile is built apart from the church of **Panayía** for protection in

Stavrós — church of the Sotíras

the event of another earthquake. The church, with its Byzantine frescoes, is usually locked, but ask in the café and the key holder might be found! The old village lies a little further up the hill.

The descent starts not far beyond here and you are soon down to **Stavrós**. We'd suggest that you keep going, *through* Stavrós and Fríkes to Kióni, then stop to explore these places on the return.

Vathí

Lying in a natural harbour, picturesque **Kióni** is a favoured port of call for holiday yachts, and there is usually a graceful flotilla in the harbour. This settlement developed as the harbour town for the mountain village of Anogí back in the 18th century. A cobbled donkey trail leads between the villages and, although it is becoming overgrown, much of it is still walkable. It starts behind the *kafénion* here in Kióni. **St John's** church, dating from 1790, was also fully repaired after the earthquake. Some traditional houses from the pre-earthquake era are still standing on the left side of the bay.

From Kióni head back to **Fríkes** — another natural and sheltered harbour, also popular with the yacht flotillas. Fishermen from both Exoyí and Stavrós settled here in the 17th century, when piracy was on the decline in the region. Fríkes Bay is a good fishing area, so the fish tavernas are well frequented. Ferries run from here to Lefkáda.

Stavrós is the largest village on the northern part of the island. There is plenty of evidence indicating that this region has been inhabited continuously since the end of the third millennium BC. The relatively recent **church of the Sotíras** (Church of the Saviour) dominates the centre; it was built in 1922 and is unusually austere inside. Opposite is a small park with a bust of Odysseus and a couple of maps, one showing the journey of Odysseus around the Mediterranean and the other tentatively identifying places on the island mentioned by Homer. Looking out from the park there is a view down to Pólis Bay. There are shops in the centre and an archaeological museum with finds from excavations in northern Itháca. This island has its own food speciality, *rovaní*, a rice cake, and it is worth checking the shops here to find it.

Take the main coastal road back now, to explore the southern part of the island. It returns you very quickly down to the neck. Notice the turn off for Píso Aetós, needed for your return to the ferry later, but keep ahead to drive towards Vathí.

Romantics on Homer's trail, wanting to visit the **Cave of the Nymphs**, need to watch out for the right turn just after passing

Dexá Beach. Be warned that there isn't much to see, and the small entrance fee covers the light from the guide's torch — if you can squeeze through the narrow entrance. It's a 2km drive along a very twisting one-lane road.

Vathí is the capital of Itháca and the only town of any significance on the southern part of the island. It lies on the southern shore of the Gulf of Mólos and is surrounded by hills. After the earthquake, houses were rebuilt in the old traditional style. In recognition, it was granted the status of 'Traditional Settlement' in 1982 — which means that all new properties must be built sympathetically. Tavernas line the quayside, so there is a good choice. The square is the hub of the town's social life, surrounded by cafés and bars. There are two museums in the middle of town, the Archaeological Museum (open 08.00-15.00, closed Mondays) and the Maritime and Folklore Museum (open 09.30-15.30, closed Sundays). The Archaeological Museum has a collection of finds, pottery, bronzes and coins, from Alalkamenós and elsewhere on the island. The small island of Lazarétto at the entrance to the port was a place of quarantine from 1668 under the Venetians and English. After union with Greece, it was converted to a jail, but was eventually destroyed by the earthquake.

Perahóri, in the hills behind Vathí, is noted for its wine, but more interesting is the old village of **Paleohóra** nearby. It's full of interesting ruins, including old churches with still-visible frescoes.

From here head back to **Píso Aetós** for the ferry.

Homer's Odyssey

Written in the 8th century BC, Homer's *Iliad* and *Odyssey* are treasured literary epics illuminating so many events in the Mycenaean era. The *Iliad* was based on the last 40 days of the 10-year Trojan War, of which Odysseus was one of the heroes. The *Odyssey* follows the journey of Odysseus, King of Itháca, on his protracted 10-year-long journey home. Poseidon, God of the Sea, was angry with Odysseus and did everything in his power to prevent him and his companions from returning. Extremely imaginative disasters and adventures befell Odysseus, slowing his return, including being imprisoned for seven years by the nymph Kalypso who took rather a fancy to him. However, Athena, Goddess of Wisdom, finally came to his aid and guided him back to his loving wife, who had spent most of the time beating off would-be suitors.

Odysseus bust in Stavrós Castle

Scholars try relentlessly to identify the places associated with Odysseus, and Itháca and Kefaloniá appear most likely. Both have ancient Mycenaean sites not found on neighbouring islands. Itháca seems to have the strongest claim, but academics are still not wholly convinced and, during our last visit, excavations were in hand on Kefaloniá's Palíki Peninsula to tie that region to Odysseus — arguing that it fits the scenic descriptions more accurately.

Homer's descriptive writing uses some really colourful phrases and his 'wine-dark seas' is one that stays with us and really does evoke the deep purple-blue seas around Kefaloniá.

A walk back in history through the area which was once part of ancient Próni touches on more tangible, recent history in the abandoned village of Asprogérakas. Most of all, you feel the freedom of the outdoors evoked by the ever-changing expansive views almost all the way through this walk.

from ag geórgios to ag paraskeví

WALK

8

Start the walk at **Ag Geórgios**: follow the concrete road (**①**) opposite the buff-coloured church; it may be signposted to Kornélos (if not, it is to the right of a vine-trellised house and parallels the main Póros road at first). The road becomes a wide, comfortable corniche track with fine views as the village is left behind. In 15-20 minutes you pass a winding **track right uphill** (**②**) to Kornélos and ancient Próni (called Paleókastro). There is debate as to whether this or the acropolis above Póros (Walk 9) was the most important Mycenaean site.

At the point where the track bends right, there is a **shrine** on the left and **Póros Gorge** lies ahead. Signs of cultivation herald your approach to civilisation, and trees shade the way. Ignore a track off right just outside **Asprogérakas**, where post-

Distance: 10.7km/6.7mi; 2h45min

Grade: easy-moderate, with 100m of ascent

Equipment: walking boots or trainers, water, sun protection, warm top and waterproof outside summer

Transport: 🚌 to/from Ag Geórgios

Refreshments: none on route, but plenty of choice at Póros Port and in Poros town; see pages 120, 127.

Alternative: Ag Geórgios to Poros: Follow the main walk to Ag Paraskeví, then continue down the track towards Poros. You pass Walk 9 coming in from the left just before the boundary sign. When the road forks, keep right. The road reverts briefly to track before it bends left in front of the Oceanis Hotel. Turn right here, down a steep concrete road, then go left along the tarmac road to Sunset Taverna — or continue down the steps on its right-hand side, to the main road in Poros (10.5km/6.6mi; 3h). Easy, mostly downhill, with one short gradual ascent; access by 🚌 — leave one either end, or ask friends to collect you: there are *no* taxis at Poros, but there *are* buses, so check timetables

Points of interest:
'ghost' villages of Asprogérakas and Anináta above it
Mycenaean Próni (Paleókastro)

earthquake buildings mark your arrival. You soon reach a **junction** (❸; **50min**) where the track ahead continues to Faniés and Skála. Stay left here (there is a **well** on the corner), to pass the village **church** — a good spot to sit and reflect.

Just past here, turn right uphill on a track which takes you looping through the other earthquake village of **Aninata**, seen on the skyline ahead. Both Asprogérakas and Aninata were once affluent villages, but became 'ghost' villages after the 1953 earthquake, when many inhabitants emigrated. At the junction past the **church** on the right, keep right to an excellent **viewpoint** (❹) at the top of the village.

Then return to the junction and go right to the red-roofed church of **Ag Paraskeví** (❺; **1h 30min**), another good viewpoint. Turn sharp left here, gently descending round the valley, back to **Asprogérakas** (❸), then retrace your steps to **Ag Geórgios** (3h).

View across the valley towards Tzanáta from the church of Ag Paraskeví

119

Remetzo Café/Bar

An unexpected haven by the sea on the edge of the port area, with a good selection of snacks. Head left, round the far side of the café, to a very pleasant and imaginative bar area among the rocks, set out like the deck of a sailing ship. It's an ideal spot for a light lunch. Sit in comfort and watch the arrival and departure of the ferries and the waves on the shingle.

Remetzo Café/Bar and one of their 'light snacks'!

REMETZO CAFÉ/BAR
Póros port
open daily €

large selection of **drinks**, including our favourite iced chocolate and, of course, cold beer and oúzo

light **snacks** with chips; huge **sandwiches**; various **salad**s, apple pie, cakes and fruit salad

restaurants

eat

Sunset Taverna (Iliovasílema)

This is a wonderful place, especially for an evening meal to watch the sunset, as it sits on the hillside with panoramic views over the port area to Póros beyond. The chef produces some delicious food, and daughter Voula acts as waitress, but there is a special treat when things calm down in the kitchen. Voula produces her guitar and sings for the diners — and she's absolutely first class. If she has one of her CDs for sale, don't hesitate to buy one. It has proved one of the best Greek recordings, with full backing, we have brought back from Greece and is professionally produced. An amazing discovery!

> **SUNSET TAVERNA**
> **above Póros port**
> **open daily in season €-€€**
>
> excellent selection of tasty Greek dishes like ***pastítsio, giouvétsi, kokkinistó;*** **fish; grills; stuffed roast pork;** ***spanakòrizo*** **(spinach with rice);** **walnut cake,** ***baklavá***

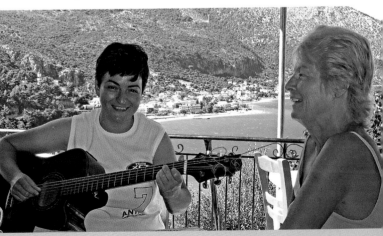

Melizanosaláta (Roasted aubergine salad)

Wrap the aubergines in foil and bake in the oven at 180°C for about 30 min until they are very soft, or microwave, minus foil, for about 10 min. (To get the distinctive smoky flavour of an authentic *melizanosaláta*, the aubergines really need to be cooked on a barbecue.)

Scoop out the flesh and blend until smooth. Add the garlic, salt and pepper, the softened and chopped pepper pieces, then the oil and lemon — slowly, so that the finished mix is firm and not sloppy.

Ingredients (for 4 people)
450 g large aubergines
1 garlic clove, crushed as creamy as possible
10 ml olive oil
10 ml lemon juice
salt & pepper
1 small pepper or pieces of different colours, briefly softened in the oven or microwave, then finely chopped

Tirosaláta (Spicy cheese dip) not illustrated

Soften the pepper briefly in the oven or microwave, then skin, de-seed and chop into small pieces. Mash the cheese. Put all the ingredients into a blender and whizz briefly. Serve in a bowl as part of a *mezé* selection.

Tirosaláta: Ingredients (for 4 people)
100g moist *féta* or other soft creamy cheese
1 red hot pepper
2 tsps olive oil
1 tsp vinegar

recipes

eat

Kounéli lemonáto (Rabbit in lemon)

Wash and dry the rabbit. Leave to marinate in the wine for a few hours. Remove the rabbit from the marinade, dry and dust with seasoned flour.

Pre-heat the oven to 180°C. Heat the oil in a pan and brown the rabbit pieces, then place them in a casserole dish.

Stir into the pan the garlic, tomato paste, flour, bay leaves, wine, salt and pepper. (Add a little extra olive oil or water if needed.) Pour this over the rabbit.

Cook for about 1 h 30 min, or until the rabbit is tender. Add the lemon juice about 10 min from the end of cooking. If the juices are still runny, add a little flour paste to thicken when adding the lemon juice.

Ingredients (for 4 people)
1 rabbit, in 4 joints
2 tbsp flour
300 ml white wine
2 tbsp tomato paste
3 tbsp olive oil
5 garlic cloves, crushed
2 bay leaves
1 lemon (juice of)
salt & black pepper

Left: A meze plate for two people to share, at the Sunset Taverna

Venture inside the vaulted tomb of a Mycenaean king who lived around the time of Homer's *Odyssey*. Then enjoy changing vistas along the valley and climb over the acropolis hill behind Póros. Much evidence of the once-great city state lies scattered nearby, but the views from the top are reward enough for the climb.

the tholos tomb above póros

WALK

View from the highest point in the walk

Start the walk at **Poros port** (**❶**): *carefully* follow the main road to **Tzanáta**, watching out for traffic on any blind bends. After 3km, as the road bends hard right, take the track off left signposted to the tholos tomb (**❷**; **1h**). You reach the **Mycenaen Tholos Tomb** 10 minutes later: dating from 1400-1350BC, it is the largest known vaulted tomb in north-western Greece.

After visiting the tomb, continue along the track for a few minutes, to a **bridge**. Cross the bridge and turn left on a track, following the river on the left. Rise to a gate and continue past a goat-watering place. A fenced goat pen now blocks the path ahead, so skirt it to the left, walking between the fence and a stream, and follow a vague path — avoiding the

See map on page 118

Distance: 8.2km/5mi; 4h

Grade: moderate-strenuous; *only recommended for confident walkers.* Overall ascent of 300m; stony underfoot in places. Possible route-finding problems, despite numbered signposts and yellow rhombus waymarks (fixed for walkers *coming from* Póros); look carefully for these if unsure.

Equipment: hiking boots, water, sun protection, warm top/waterproof in early/late season

Transport: 🚌 or 🚗 to/from Poros port — or with friends to Tzanáta: alight just beyond the track off left, on a blind corner, signposted to the tholos tomb.

Refreshments: none on route, but plenty of choice back at Póros Port and in the town; see pages 120, 127.

Points of interest:
Mycenaean tholos tomb (free entry; open until 15.00; closed Mondays) remnants of the ancient acropolis of Próni on top of the hill behind Póros

edge of the gully. Continue on the path rising to the right, which passes the bole of an ancient olive tree and runs into a stony field (**1h25min**). Stay ahead, briefly skirting the top edge of the goat fence. Then turn left, steeply uphill, through a wide, stony

Mycenaean tholos tomb

area. The path then heads right, levels out somewhat at the top of the rise and leads into another large stony field (**1h40min**). Keep left along the edge of this area to continue ahead on a strong path. (You are heading north-northeast in the direction of the Póros Gorge, although you cannot see it yet.) After the path descends to cross the head of the gully on the left (**1h55min**), start to head more to the right.

Keep ahead past a signpost, to reach an area of storm-damaged **plane trees** (❸; **2h**). Walk between a fallen plane tree down left and a **semi-circular stone bench**, then go right uphill (perhaps skirting another fallen plane tree), towards **another semi-circular stone bench**. Continue uphill to the left of the stone bench, *even where it looks as if branches block the way.* Soon you rise onto a track with a **signpost**; cross straight over and stay uphill on the path. The path winds through holm oaks, heading more to the left of the slope, and at least there is some shade.

Don't forget to check for the **yellow diamonds** if you are unsure of the route in places. When you approach a **rocky barrier** (❹; **2h30min**), you will see a path running ahead through the barrier, but *turn sharp left before the rocks,* to continue uphill and cross back over the stony slope you just climbed. Rise to a **signposted crossing path** and stay left. Nearly at the top, you reach a **signposted path junction**, where you turn *sharp right* towards Póros. (You could go straight ahead here to seek out remnants of rocks/walls of **ancient Próni** (⑤) and return to this point to continue.)

In a minute you rise to the highest point in the walk and first view of Póros through the trees. Descend ahead, to a ledge where the path goes right and downhill. When the path starts to level out, continue alongside a **wire fence** above the field below on the left. Join a track and head downhill. This stony track meets a track coming from the left. After a steep concreted descent, ignore another track joining from the left. When you meet a **tarmac road** (⑥), turn left and immediately pass the **Póros boundary sign** on the left. When the road forks, keep right. The road bends left in front of the Oceanis Hotel. Turn right here, down the steep concrete road, then go left along the tarmac road to **Sunset Taverna** (see page 121). Continue down the steps on its right-hand side, to join the main Skála/Póros road. Turn left to **Póros port** (**4h**).

Taverna Tsívras *illustrated*

Less flamboyant than its neighbour, but with much better home-cooked food, the second of two

> **TAVERNA TSÍVRAS**
> just above Póros port
> open daily in season €-€€
> local **Greek dishes** and **fresh fish**; good **house wine**

tavérnas uphill from the port in the direction of Skála is our choice down in the port area.

restaurants

eat

Keftédes (Meatballs)

Mix all the ingredients thoroughly for a few minutes, but add the egg gradually, as the mix needs to be firm not sloppy. Divide into 16 table-

tennis size balls and coat lightly with the flour.

Heat 1cm depth olive oil/rape seed oil in a frying pan. Cook the meatballs over a medium heat until they are brown all over and just cooked but moist in the centre.

Drain on kitchen paper and serve with mashed potatoes and a selection of vegetables.

Ingredients (for 4 people)
500 g lean minced beef
1 medium onion, grated
1/2 tsp dried oregano
1/2 tsp dried mint
1 tsp dried parsley (or 2 tbsp of finely chopped fresh)
1 tbsp red wine (optional)
1 thick slice of white bread, dunked in cold water (squeeze out water and remove crust)
1 small egg
salt & black pepper
3 tbsp flour for coating

Skordaliá (Garlic dip) *ingredients and photograph opposite*

Boil the potatoes in their skins. When cool, discard the skins and mash well. Mash the garlic into a creamy paste and combine thoroughly with the potato. (Taste as you go, as this can be quite strongly flavoured. You may even wand to add more garlic!)

Gradually blend in the olive oil, lemon juice and salt and pepper, until the mixture is creamy but not sloppy.

recipes

eat

Fasolátha (Bean soup)

A Greek favourite which can be made quickly using tinned beans. *If using tinned beans,* heat the oil in a large pan and soften the onion, carrot and celery. Add the garlic and chopped tomatoes, cook a little longer, then add the stock and bring to the boil. Drain and rinse the tinned beans and add to the mixture. Stir and heat again to serve.

If using dried beans, soak overnight in plenty of water. Then strain and put in a pan, well covered with water, bring to the boil and strain. Put the beans in a large pan with all the other ingredients, bring to the boil, cover and simmer for 1 h.

Skordaliá goes well with *tsigaridiá,* Kefalonian 'wild greens' (see page 13).

Skordaliá: Ingredients (for 4 people)

450 g large floury potatoes
4 garlic cloves
50 ml olive oil
1 tbsp lemon juice
salt & pepper

Ingredients (for 2-3 people)

250 g dried white beans (or
   2 x 300 g tins of cannelli
   beans — 360 g drained)
2 small carrots, peeled and
   thinly diced
1 small onion, chopped
1 garlic clove, crushed
2 small stalks of celery,
   chopped
200 ml chopped tomatoes
2 tbsp olive oil
600 ml stock (1 chicken stock
   cube); add more water if
   needed during cooking

Spread over a large area of hillside, it's difficult now to imagine old Skála being the large and thriving village it was only recently. As you wander around the atmospheric ruins, be aware that they are unstable and best viewed with care. A few properties are being rebuilt by families — for what appears to be holiday letting.

old skála

WALK

The walk starts in **Plátanos Square** (**❶**), above the shore, at the bottom of the main street through **Skála**.* Head inland, ascending the main street, and stay ahead at crossroads on the edge of the village. After around 15-20 minutes of steady uphill walking, the route levels out. Wandering along this country road, it's difficult to spot the location of the old village on the hillside ahead. The road bends almost parallel with the

Distance: 9.2km/5.8mi; 3h15min

Grade: moderate, with a climb of some 160m — or more, if you clamber around the ruins

Equipment: hiking boots, water, sun protection, warm top/waterproof in early/late season

Transport: 🚌, 🚗 car or taxi to Skála centre (there are parking areas near the shore)

Refreshments: Taverna Kelári in Old Skala (open all day in season) and plenty of choice in Skála

Points of interest:
Roman villa foundations near Skála
ruins of old Skála

coast over to your right and passes two **water storage tanks** on the left. Not long afterwards, at a junction, stay left (**❷**; **30min**).

Descend into a dip and, when you come to a track crossing the road diagonally, keep ahead, to start the climb up to old Skála. Ignore tracks left and right, and stay on the road. You pass a track heading downhill to the left (**❸**; **1h15min**); this is the return route. A couple of bends further on, just after a track joins from the right on the bend, you come to the first ruin in **old Skála** (**1h20min**). The next ruin, on the left, just before the

*Nearby are the foundations of a **Roman villa** with mosaics still intact: the easiest way to get there is to follow the road behind the beach past Milos restaurant, then turn right through a small car parking area. It costs nothing to see the mosaics.

electricity stanchion, was the only house in the village with electricity. Further along on the right is an **olive press** with the rusting remains of a diesel engine (made in Bolton by R Fielding). Just before the olive press, on the same side, were the village shops and tavernas and, on the far side, the doctor's house with a *kafénion* next door. The route ahead leads to Faniés, and the walk will continue left downhill.

But first turn sharp right up the track above the village — to **Taverna Kelári**, with an adventurous Greek menu (beef steak or chicken in brandy; interesting starters and fish dishes such as 'Shrimps Old Skala' with red sauce and flavoured with ouzo) and superb views. From there continue ahead to a small ancient **amphitheatre** (**④**) with more good views over the sea.

Then return to the junction and continue by crossing the road and heading downhill to the surviving **bell-tower, cemetery** and newly rebuilt **church of Archángelos** (**⑤**), which is accessible. Lower down the hillside is the **spring** and **wash-house**, a focal point of village life for the women and village gossip.

Soon turn sharp left, to head back below the village. Watch for a path forking left: this takes you to the **lower spring and**

wash-house. (Beware of the roof which was damaged by a boulder during the earthquake.) Return along the same path to the track to continue. A track joining sharply uphill from the right was a major route from the village to Moúnda Beach. After passing an electricity sub-station on the left, look off the track, uphill, for the **ruined church and cemetery of the Virgin Mary** (**⑥**), behind which is another **olive press** and **grape-treading tanks**. Rejoin the track.

Soon you meet the road up to the village (the 1h15min-point of the outward walk). Turn right downhill and retrace the outward route back to **Skála** (**3h15min**).

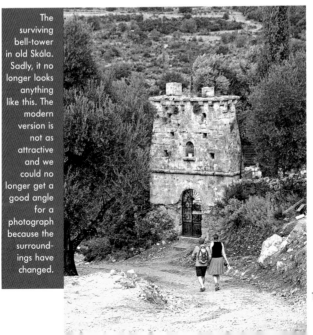

The surviving bell-tower in old Skála. Sadly, it no longer looks anything like this. The modern version is not as attractive and we could no longer get a good angle for a photograph because the surroundings have changed.

The Old Village

On the main street, next to the bakery and opposite the church and large white council office (with flag), this taverna has some unusual starters — like 'kagianas' (fried egg with sausage in a spicy tomato sauce with feta.

> **THE OLD VILLAGE**
> **Skála, open daily in season** €-€€
>
> some **mains: chicken *tigania*** (chicken bites with peppers and lemon in mustard sauce); ***roumeliotiko*** (marinated grilled goat with tomatoes in pita bread; **mama's lamb** (with giant beans, herbs and tomato sauce)

Ta Pitharía

Tucked along a street on the north side of the church, parallel with the main street. Some amusing cartoons adorn the walls, the food is good, and there is a relaxing atmosphere. A well presented appetiser comes with the bread, and a pleasant touch is hot towels with the bill.

> **TA PITHARIA**
> **Skála; open daily in season** €-€€
>
> traditional Greek specialities, like **lamb *kleftiko*** and ***mousakás*** in a clay bowl
>
> excellent **baklavá** with ice cream

restaurants

eat

Giouvétsi (Youvétsi) (Beef and *manéstra*)

This is a popular dish made with beef and the rice-like pasta, *manéstra* (see page 11).

Pre-heat the oven to 180°C. Dust the meat lightly with the flour and brown in some of the hot olive oil. Place in a large casserole.

Add the rest of the olive oil to the pan and soften the onions. Stir in the tomato paste, crushed tomatoes, oregano, cumin, salt and pepper, and the water. Heat and place with the meat in the casserole. Cook in the oven for 1 h.

Then add the *manéstra*, and top up with water if necessary to prevent the contents drying out as the pasta absorbs the liquid. Check the liquid level at times during cooking.

Cook a further 50 min to 1 h — or until the meat is tender and the pasta soft.

This dish is served in individual clay bowls in Greece — with a selection of green vegetables or a mixed salad.

Photo: *Giouvétsi* at Tzívras (see page 41)

Ingredients (for 4 people)
750 g beef or lamb, cut in
   2.5 cm cubes
300 g *manéstra* (I mainly use
   métrio — medium).
2 onions, chopped
2 garlic cloves, crushed
1 tbsp tomato paste
1 400 g tin crushed tomatoes
500 ml beef or lamb stock
   (chicken is fine, use 1 stock
   cube)
1 tsp dried oregano
1 tsp cumin
3 tbsp olive oil
1 tbsp flour for coating the
   meat
salt & black pepper

recipes

eat

Kolokithokeftédes (Courgette balls)

Grate the courgettes and squeeze out as much liquid as possible. Add all the other ingredients, except the flour, and mix well. Bind together with enough olive oil so that the mixture holds firmly together. Then form

into table-tennis size balls and lightly coat the balls in the seasoned flour.

Heat a 2 cm depth of oil in a pan and fry the balls, turning to make sure they are evenly cooked, for about 6 min. Drain on kitchen paper and serve as a starter or part of a *mezé*.

Ingredients (for 2-3 people)
500 g courgettes
1 medium onion, grated
100 g hard cheese — *kefalotiri, graviera* or cheddar, grated
30 g breadcrumbs
70 g plain flour
50 ml olive oil (or enough to bind)
1 tsp dried parsley or 1 tbsp fresh, finely chopped
1 tsp dried dill or 1 tbsp fresh, finely chopped
salt & black pepper
1 tbsp seasoned flour.

recipes

eat

The name of the dish below derives from the pot *'stámna'* in which it's cooked. Originally the lid was sealed with a flour paste, and the pot was buried in the hot ash from a fire to cook.

Stamnáki

Pre-heat the oven to 180°C. Heat the olive oil in a large pan and soften the onion. Stir in the garlic, spices and black pepper, then add the meat coated in seasoned flour to the pan and brown.

Stir in the wine, the stock cubes (dissolved in the water) and the tomatoes. Bring to the boil and transfer to a casserole dish.

Cook in the oven for 1 h, then add the potatoes and carrots. Add the green beans to the casserole in a further 20 min.

Allow 2 h overall cooking time — or until the meat is tender and the vegetables cooked, adding extra water if needed.

Sprinkle over the cheese and leave in the oven a little longer to melt. Then divide into individual serving bowls and serve.

Ingredients (for 2 people)

500 g beef or lamb (not a cheap cut), cut into 2.5 cm chunks
50 ml olive oil
1 onion, chopped
3 garlic cloves, crushed
1 400 g tin chopped tomatoes
2 large potatoes, cut into pieces
2 carrots, thickly sliced
110 g green beans, sliced
2 beef stock cubes
200 ml water
160 ml red or white wine
1 pinch of ground cloves
black pepper (salt is in the stock cubes and the cheese)
1 tsp paprika
2 tbsp flour
50 g *fetá* or crumbly Lancashire cheese for the topping

Not many people visiting Greece on a casual basis find the Greek language easy to get to grips with. The first obstacle is the Greek alphabet itself. It uses a fair number of characters not represented in the Latin alphabet. In many situations, particularly with place names, road signs and even menus, it is deemed important to change the Greek over to the Latin alphabet to make the names more understandable to foreigners. Unfortunately, there is no definitive or official way to change Greek letters to their Latin equivalent for some of the reasons outlined below. This itself just adds to the confusion, as you will see.

Learning one or two of the pitfalls shown here should help with reading menus in tavernas and with some pronunciations.

The trouble with 'g': On the face of it, this seems a fairly straightforward transliteration. The problem is that 'g' is pronounced as 'y' when preceding 'i' or 'e', but as 'g' in other instances. So a word like *gemistá* (meaning 'stuffed', as in tomatoes or peppers}, is often written as *yemistá* — the way it is pronounced. *Ágios,* meaning 'saint', is another common word regularly mispronounced by visitors. Again the 'g' has a 'y' sound, so it sounds like *áyios.*

The trouble with 'mp': Since the letter 'b' is pronounced as a 'v', it leaves the alphabet without a 'b' sound. To overcome this, a combination of letters, 'mp' is used. This combination is pronounced as 'b' at the start of a word, but as 'mb' anywhere else in the word. The Greek word *mpampou* is a classic illustration. That is how it might be written as a conversion from the Greek alphabet — or equally, it could be written *bambou*. From here it is only a small step to recognise it as 'bamboo'. The mp/mb confusion is commonly noticed on the menu with

GREEK

lamb chops, often seen as 'lamp' chops — which raises a smile with visitors (… but the Greeks would pronounce it as 'lamb' anyway).

'Lamp' cutlets

The trouble with 'nt': This is another combination of letters which is pronounced as a normal 'd' at the beginning of a word and 'nd' elsewhere. It crops up in words like *ntomátes* (tomatoes), which can also appear as *domátes*. This combination is used when a hard 'd' is required, because the 'd' in the Greek alphabet is pronounced as a soft 'd', almost like a 'th'. The word for two, *deo*, for example, is pronounced *theo*.

There are one or two other letter combinations with special pronunciations, but those above are the ones most commonly encountered and the most useful ones to learn.

In the menu and shopping listings, we have used the transliteration that points the way towards the correct pronunciation, but remember that the stress (´) is important too!

CONVERSION TABLES

Weights		Volume		Oven temperatures		
						gas
10 g	1/2 oz	15 ml	1 tbsp	°C	°F	mark
25 g	1 oz	55 ml	2 fl oz	140°C	275°F	1
50 g	2 oz	75 ml	3 fl oz	150°C	300°F	2
110 g	4 oz	150 ml	1/4 pt	170°C	325°F	3
200 g	7 oz	275 ml	1/2 pt	180°C	350°F	4
350 g	12 oz	570 ml	1 pt	190°C	375°F	5
450 g	1 lb	1 l	1-3/4 pt	200°C	400°F	6
700 g	1 lb 8 oz	1.5 l	2-1/2 pt	220°C	425°F	7
900 g	2 lb			230°C	430°F	8
1.35 g	3 lb			240°C	475°F	9

MENU ITEMS

akinós sea urchin

aláti salt

angoúri cucumber

arakás peas

arní lamb

  kokkinistó in tomoto sauce

  kléftiko in filo parcel with veg/ cheese

  lemonáto in herb sauce with lemon

brizóles chops

psitó roast

áspro white

áspro krasí white wine

astakós lobster

atherina small, whitebait-like fish

bakaliáros cod

baklavá filo pastry, nuts soaked in syrup

bámies okra, ladies fingers

barboúni fish similar to red mullet

biftékia mince done as a beefburger

bira beer

bouzákia grilled lamb or goat

briám similar to ratatouille

brizóla chop

deípno dinner

dolmádes vine leaves, rolled and stuffed with mince and rice

domátes tomatoes

  yemistés stuffed with rice, herbs and maybe mince

elaiólado olive oil

eliés olives

Ellinikós kafés Greek coffee (never with milk)

  glykós sweet

  métrios medium sweet

  skétos plain, simple (no sugar)

fasolákia green beans

fáva yellow pea purée

féta feta cheese

  saganáki sto foúrno oven-baked feta with tomatoes and peppers

filéto filet

fráoules strawberries

fréska froúta fresh fruit

galaktoboúreko filo/ custard sweet

galopoúla turkey

galéos cod

  me skordaliá with garlic dip

garídes prawns (pronounced garithes)

g(y)emistá stuffed

g(y)iaoúrti yoghurt

  me méli with honey

g(y)ígantes giant butter beans in sauce

giouvétsi veal in a clay pot with manéstra

glyka dessert ('sweet')

g(y)úros meat from large skewer

haloúmi cheese

halvás sesame/ sugar sweet

hoirinó pork

hoiriní brizóla pork chop

horiátiki saláta Greek salad

hortofágos vegetarian

hoúmous hummus

imám baíldi stuffed aubergine

kafés coffee

frappé iced

me gála with milk

kakáo hot chocolate

kakaviá fish soup

kalamári squid

karidiá walnuts

karpoúzi watermelon

kataífi pastry, like shredded wheat strands, soaked in syrup

katálogos menu

  krasión wine list

katsíki goat

kávouras boiled crab

kimá mince

keftédes fried meatballs

kléftiko see *arní kléftiko*

kolokithákia

  tiganitá fried

kolokithokeftédes fried courgette balls

kokkinistó veal in tomato sauce

kokteil cocktail

kondosoúvli spiced port on a spit

koniák cognac

kotolétes cutlets

kotópoulo chicken

koukiá broad beans

kounéli rabbit

krasí wine

  áspro or *lefkó* white

  kókkino red

  rozé rosé

krokétes croquettes

kserotigana (thiples) deep-friend pastry

ksifías swordfish

ksúdi vinegar (pronounced kseethi)

ládi oil

lákano cabbage

loukániko sausage

loukoumádes honey-soaked batter balls

makarónia spaghetti me kimá bolognaise ('with mince')

manéstra rice-like pasta

manitária mushrooms

marídes small fish (like whitebait)

maroúli lettuce

melekoúni see *pastéli*

méli honey

melitzána aubergine

melitzánosaláta aubergine dip

mesimerianó lunch

mezédes starters (*mezés* for short)

míla apples

moskári beef or veal

mousakás moussaka

múdia mussels

neró water

nes instant coffee

oktapódi octopus

omeléta omelette

orektiká first course, starters

oúzo aniseed spirit

pagákia ice (cubes)

pagotó ice cream

païdákia lamb chops

papoutsákia half aubergines stuffed with mince, tomato & onions, with a cheese topping

pásta cake, pastry

pastéli sesame and honey bars

pastítsio baked meat and pasta dish

patátes potatoes (often synonymous with chips in tavernas)

tiganités chips (full description)

patzária beetroot cooked with its leaves

pepóni melon

pipéri pepper

piperiés peppers yemistés stuffed

with rice and meat

pita pita bread

pítsa pizza

portokáli oranges

proinó breakfast

psári fish

psarotavérna fish taverna

psetó roast

psomí bread

retsína resinated wine

revithia chickpeas

revithokeftédes fried chickpea balls

rígani oregano

rúzi rice (pronounced reezee)

rúzogalo rice pudding

saganáki fried cheese starter

saláta salad

saligária snails yiáxni in a casserole with tomato sauce

sándouitz sandwich

sardéles sardines

seftaliá home-made sausage

sikóti liver

sikotariá fried liver and kidney

skordaliá garlic/ mashed potato dip

skórdo garlic

soúpa soup

soutzoukákia spicy

meat rolls

souvláki meat on skewer

spanakópita spinach pie in filo

spetzofáï sausage and peppers in spicy sauce

stafúlia grapes

ste soúvla spit roast

stifádo meat stew with shallots

sto foúrno baked in the oven

strídia oysters

talagoútes small thick (sweet) pancakes

taramosaláta fish roe paste dip

thalasiná seafood

tiganitá/és/ó (all variations mean 'fried')

tirí cheese

tirokeftédes cheese balls

tirópita cheese pie

tirosaláta spicy cheese dip

tónnos tuna

tost toast

tsáï tea

tzatzíki yoghurt, garlic, cucumber dip

vradinó evening meal

vrastó boiled

yaoúrti yoghurt

yemistá/és/ó (all variations mean 'stuffed')

youvétsi veal stew with *manéstra*

zambon ham

zákari sugar

zesté sokoláta hot chocolate

SHOPPING TERMS
general

bottle *boukáli*

kilo *kiló*

half-kilo *misó kiló*

carrier bag *sakoúla*

allspice *bakári* (whole or ground)

apples *méla*

apricot *veríkoko*

aubergine *melitzána*

bananas *banánes*

basil *vasilikós*

bay leaf *dáfne*

beans, french *fasolákia*

beans, broad *koukiá*

beef *moskári*

beer *bíra*

bread *psomí*

bread (olive) *elioté*

butter *voútero*

cabbage *lákano*

cake *pásta*

carrots *karóta*

cheese *tirí*

cherries *kerásia*

chestnut *kastaniá*

chicken *kotópoulo*

chickpeas *revíthia*

chocolate *kakáo*

chop *brizóla*

cinnamon *kanéla*

coffee *kafé*

  instant *nes*

courgettes *kolokithákia*

cream *kréma*

cucumber *angoúri*

cutlets *kotolétes*

dips

  aubergine *melitzánosaláta*

  fish roe paste *taramosaláta*

  garlic/mashed potato *skordaliá*

  spicy cheese *tirosaláta*

  yoghurt/garlic/cucumber *tzatzíki*

eggs *avgá*

feta cheese *féta*

filet *filéto*

fish *psári*

  cod, dried *bakaliáros*

  cod, fresh *galéos*

  sword *ksifías*

  tuna *tónnos*

  whitebait-type *marídes*

flour *alévri*

fresh *fréska*

frozen *katepsigméno*

fruit *froúta*

garlic *skórdo*

grapes *stafélia*

ham *zambón*

honey *méli*

ice

  cubes *pagákia*

  cream *pagotó*

lamb *arní*

lettuce *maroúli*

liver *sikóti*

margarine *margaríni*

meat *kréas*

  on a skewer, for barbecuing *souvláki*

melon (water) *karpoúzi*

melon *pepóni*

milk *gála*

mince *kimás*

mushrooms *manitária*

mussels *múdia*

octopus *oktapódi*

oil *ládi*

  olive *elaiólado*

olives *eliés*

onions *kremédia*

oranges *portokáli*

oregano *rígani*

oysters *strídia*

parsley *maïdanós*

pastry *pastá*

peach *rodákino*

peas *arakás*

pepper *pipéri*

peppers *piperiés*

pork *hoirinó*

potatoes *patátes*

prawns or shrimps *garídes*

rabbit *kounéli*

rice *piláfi*

rosemary *dendrolívano*

salad *saláta*

salt *aláti*

sardines *sardélles*

sausage *loukániko*

  home-made *seftaliá*

seafood *thalasiná*

snails *saligária*

soup *soúpa*

spaghetti *makarónia*

spinach *spanáki*

squid *kalamária*

sugar *zákari*

strawberries *fráoules*

tea *tsáï*

tomatoes *domátes*

turkey *galopoúla*

veal *moskári*

vinegar *ksúdi* (pronounced *kseethi*)

walnuts *karídes* (pronounced *kareethi*)

water *neró*

wine *krasí*

  white *áspero krasí*

  red *kókkino krasí*

  rosé *rozé krasí*

yoghurt *yiaoúrti*

bold type: photograph; *italic type:* map

INDEX

Fifth edition © 2019
Published by Sunflower Books
PO Box 36061, London SW7 3WS
www.sunflowerbooks.co.uk

ISBN 978-1-85691-520-5

Cover photograph: Old Valsamáta, passing the ruined barber's shop (Walk 3)
Photographs: Brian and Eileen Anderson
Acknowledgements: see page 8
Maps: adapted by the authors and Sunflower Books (original sources: Road
    Editions and OpenStreetMap)
Series design: Jocelyn Lucas
Cookery editor: Marina Bayliss
A CIP catalogue record for this book is available from the British Library.
Printed and bound in England: Short Run Press

Before you go ...
log on to
www.sunflowerbooks.co.uk
and click on '**updates**', to see if we have been notified of any changes to the
routes or restaurants.

When you return ...
do let us know if any routes have changed because of road-building, storm
damage or the like. Have any of our restaurants closed — or any new ones
opened *on the route of the walk*? (Not Argostóli restaurants, please; these
books are not intended to be complete restaurant guides!)

Send your comments to info@sunflowerbooks.co.uk